BEAUTY AND THE BEAST

BEAUTY AND THE BEAST

STEWART ANDREW MCDOWALL

ISBN: 978-93-5420-332-9

Published: 1920

LECTOR HOUSE LLP
E-MAIL: lectorpublishing@gmail.com

BEAUTY AND THE BEAST

AN ESSAY IN EVOLUTIONARY AESTHETIC

BY

STEWART A. MCDOWALL, B.D.

Chaplain and Assistant Master at Winchester College
Author of *Evolution and the Need of Atonement,
Evolution and Spiritual Life, Evolution and
the Doctrine of the Trinity,* etc.

1920

For verily all men by nature were but vain who had no perception of God, and from the good things that are seen they
gained not power to know him that is, neither by giving heed to
the works did they recognise the artificer; but either fire, or wind,
or swift air, or circling stars, or raging water, or luminaries of
heaven, they thought to be gods that rule the world. And if it was
through delight in their beauty that they took them to be gods, let
them know how much better than these is their Sovereign Lord;
for the first author of beauty created them: but if it was through
astonishment at their power and influence, let them understand
from them how much more powerful is he that formed them; for
from the greatness of the beauty even of created things in like proportion does man form the image of their first maker. But yet for
these men there is but small blame, for they too peradventure do
but go astray while they are seeking God and desiring to find him.
For living among his works they make diligent search, and they
yield themselves up to sight, because the things that they look
upon are beautiful. But again even they are not to be excused. For
if they had power to know so much, that they should be able to
explore the course of things, how is it that they did not sooner find
the Sovereign Lord of these his works?

Wisdom xiii. 1-9.

PREFACE.

I wish to take this opportunity of expressing my gratitude to Mrs R. B. Goodden and Mr R. M. Y. Gleadowe for the help they have given me in writing this book. With Mrs Goodden the theory was discussed point by point, and her criticisms and suggestions are largely responsible for the final shaping of the argument, as well as for an important development of the theory. To Mr Gleadowe I am indebted for some useful hints, which led to a partial rearrangement of the material, by which the form of the book has been greatly improved.

S. A. McD.

WINTON,
October 1919.

CONTENTS

Page

- PREFACE. vi
- INTRODUCTION. 1
- PART I: THE THEORY. .8
- PART II: BEAUTY IN EVOLUTION. 23
- CONCLUSION. 29
- APPENDIX: ART FORMS IN DEVELOPMENT. 32

INTRODUCTION.

Are we to look at the Beautiful with our feet firmly planted on the Natural, or are we to look at the Natural from the apparently precarious height of the Beautiful? This, after all, is the dilemma of aesthetic, slow though men have been to realise it. As we read the history of Aesthetic Theory we are puzzled by the tentativeness and the uncertainty even of those philosophers who played the greatest part in moulding human thought, until it dawns on us that, idealist though they might be in all else, in this they were unconsciously disloyal to their own systems, being in some measure materialist.

An attempt to form a philosophy of religion which should start from the generally accepted facts of biological science and pass, through the common experiences of personal relationship, to the ultimate problems of Godhead and manhood, left at the close a keen sense of something lacking—something more than the lack of unity and balance inevitable in work written and published step by step. I had tried to find in Love, which is the very nature of Godhead, an essential impulse towards creation. It was clear that this creation must be the creation of something *new*, if it were to be justified; and the conclusion which forced itself upon me was that the creation of personal beings fulfilled this demand.

Yet an unsatisfied sense remained either that even the experience of love reciprocated by fresh personal beings could not be new for God with that utter newness which belief in Him as Transcendent and Perfect required, or else that His experience was not always perfect. At any rate something that would make this newness self-evident was missing. Something vital had clearly been left out. The one thing of which no account had been taken was Beauty; and I began to consider whether this missing something, all-pervading yet intangible, was not Beauty itself. And in Beauty I seemed to find what I had missed.

To Aesthetic has generally been assigned the fate of Cinderella. Her uglier sisters, Epistemology and Metaphysic, have monopolised the court invitations, for the most part. Might she not, after all, be destined to marry the Prince? A little thought made it clear that, properly arrayed, she would bid fair to outshine the others. This book is not an effort to dress her in a new fashion. Fairy godmother I cannot claim to be, nor have I a magic wand. I shall only try to strip off some of the rags, leaving her, like Psyche, to proclaim her own loveliness.

It is not my intention to give a systematic account of the development of aesthetic theory. Such books as Dr Bosanquet's *History of Aesthetic*, and the historical portion of Croce's *Aesthetic*, from which works the following summary is chiefly derived, fortunately make the task unnecessary. Nor does any detailed criticism of the work of others fall within the scope of the present essay. My aim is merely to suggest an idea, avoiding technicalities as far as I may, and then to link it up with the Christian idea of God on the one hand, and with the development of the human soul on the other. The very briefest note on the course of speculation concerning Art and Beauty will suffice to introduce the point of view that I wish to suggest, which is that Beauty must be a first and not a last consideration for metaphysic. To advocate this is to turn his own weapon against Croce; but that is inevitable. Croce claims that Beauty is the expression of that intuition of Reality which constitutes the first stage of knowledge; but the philosophy of Croce is anti-metaphysical. Since many, while agreeing with the great and original discovery involved in his affirmation, must disagree profoundly with his negation, it follows of necessity that sooner or later they will endeavour to hoist him with his own petard.

Aesthetic theories show a steady and yet very remarkable change in the views of philosophers concerning Art and even Beauty itself. The Greeks tended, on the whole, to regard Art as mere imitation. Thus, at best, the beauty produced by artistic creation was inferior, because second-hand; in fact, as Plato argued, the artist's representation was really third-hand, for there is first the idea, then the concrete individual object, then the representation. Stress was laid on harmony, rhythm, order, as being indicative of the homogeneity of an ideal world and therefore admirable. But, being an incomplete reproduction of nature[1], art could have no primary importance. It might be evil or good, in its own degree; and from the moral standpoint it might be judged, for the beautiful and the good are not completely distinguished. Being so judged, it was found wanting. It is one of the tragedies of thought that the beauty-loving Plato should have been driven to formulate a theory which is the negation of art, because it seemed to him that art was simply the false endeavouring to masquerade as the true. In Aristotle we find the beginnings of a freer idea. Symbolism in art is implicitly recognised, and there is some escape, though not much, from the moralistic bond; some dawning conception, though not much, of the concrete expressiveness of artistic creation. In the Middle Ages the mystical symbolic conception, characteristic of Plotinus, was developed. Symmetry and rhythm are beautiful because they symbolise reason and divinity, and relate the human soul, through the perception of order, to the divine which created that order. St Thomas Aquinas even goes so far as to say that in beauty desire is quieted[2]—presumably because satisfied. We shall be led to disagree profoundly with this statement.

Of Vico (1725), to whom Croce acknowledges so great a debt, we will only here say that he was the discoverer of the creative intuition, and this discovery entitles him to the honourable position of first founder of a coherent theory of aesthetic. Vico was primarily concerned with the nature of poetry. He showed that poetry was a 'moment' of the spiritual consciousness, by which a man was brought into contact with reality—that it represented a stage of knowledge *before* reflection (and was therefore an intuition) and that it expressed this knowledge (and was therefore creative); while it was distinct from feeling, and therefore free from the stigma which Plato attached to it, and which led to his banishing it from

[1] Bosanquet, *Hist. Aesth.* p. 18.
[2] *Ibid.* p. 148.

his *Republic.*

> Men first *feel* without being aware; they then *become aware* with troubled and affected soul; finally they reflect with pure mind. This dignity is the *Principle of the poetical feelings*, which are formed by the senses of *passions* and of *affections*, as distinct from the *philosophical feelings*, which are formed from *reflection by reasoning*. Hence the philosophical feelings approach more to truth, the more they rise to *universals*; the poetical feelings are more certain the more they approach to *particulars*.[3]

Poetry is thus placed on the imaginative plane, says Professor Wildon Carr, as distinct from the intellective, and this imaginative plane, or as Croce calls it, degree, is furnished with positive value.

By Kant we first find the problem of aesthetic faced boldly and at close quarters. Kant's thought had led him to the formulation of two Critiques, the one dealing with the world of abstract reason, the other with the world of concrete, practical experience; and no systematic bond yet existed between them. The unity of life itself made such a dualism intolerable, and Kant sought the unifying medium in aesthetic judgment, for judgment is pre-eminently a synthesis. The domain of aesthetic consciousness, if purely subjective by Kant's interpretation, is yet clearly determined. It furnishes decisions on the quality, the quantity and the relation of those objects with which practical experience makes us acquainted, and with whose existence the intellect is occupied. Yet beauty is for Kant subjective, devoid of abstract conceptions, pleasing without interest, destitute of content; though he fails in achieving more than a verbal consistency in this matter[4]. Subjective or not, however, it is symbolic of the moral order, and owes its apparent rationality to the Order which it symbolises. No doubt it is through the doctrine of symbolism that Kant is led on to his discussion of the sublime as another species of the aesthetic judgment, yet more subjective, yet more abstract.

With Schelling we reach the stage of philosophical appreciation of the objectivity of beauty; and, with this objectivity, of the relation of beauty to historical continuity, both in its own expression in the mind of man, and in the sequence of objective episodes. The artist recognises the eternal idea in an individual, and expresses it outwardly, transforming the individual into a world apart, into a species, into an eternal idea[5]. The divine, successively expressing itself through man, gives a unity and absoluteness to all reality; and reality is the object of the aesthetic judgment.

We have not stayed to discuss, or even state, the many definitions of the Beautiful that have been given. Neither have we attempted to represent the contribution of countless writers to the problem. Our only object in this brief page of summary has been to indicate the changing trend of thought.

The Greeks reared their philosophic system on an unstable foundation, be-

---

[3] G. Vico, *Scienza nuova seconda, Elementi liii,* quoted in Croce's *Aesthetic.*
[4] Bosanquet, *Hist. Aesth.* p. 267, *seq.*
[5] Croce, *Aesthetic,* trs. Ainslie, p. 303.

cause they looked on Beauty as mere imitation. For them Art mimics life as crudely as a company of strolling players at a country fair mimics the doings of the great. Art is dramatic rather than true.

But with less rigorous and honest minds than Plato's the instinctive love of beauty weighed more strongly. Beauty was, at highest, too ennobling to be wholly false; it must at least symbolise the true. And when a more disciplined thought was once more turned upon Reality, without beauty the world seemed dual—hard and cold, with theory and practice divorced. The only bond appeared to lie in the region of the judgment of values, itself essentially aesthetic. Men born out of due time there were who showed here and there flashes of deeper insight before Kant's systematisation was effected, but to them came only sporadic glimpses of the truth. These for the most part were men deeply versed in the life and soul of man—the Dantes, the Shakespeares, the Goethes. Only one was pre-eminent in the realm of pure thought—Giambattista Vico. With other thinkers the tide rose and fell alternately, yet always moved from the neap of Platonism towards the spring.

Then, at the end, in our own time, Benedetto Croce set himself to formulate the first adequate theory of the Aesthetic.

The importance of Beauty to any system of philosophy that could pretend to completeness had been more and more recognised. It was left for Croce to grasp the truth that Beauty is not judgment, but expression: the expression of the intuition which is our first contact with Reality; and that Aesthetic is the science of expressive activity. Given this first movement of the spirit, the other modes of approach to Reality follow—or rather are involved, since no temporal series is concerned.

Croce's philosophy as a whole, and especially his extension of the logical *a priori* synthesis on which it is founded, is difficult to grasp; and for the sake of those who may not have made acquaintance with his own exposition or with Professor Wildon Carr's summary, a brief discussion of one or two salient points may be forgiven. It is only fair to state, however, that it is not possible to give a really short and clear *résumé* that will do justice to the most interesting and elusive of modern philosophies.

We may begin by explaining what Croce means by an intuition, what he means by the *a priori* synthesis, and what part the relation of the double degree plays in his system.

When you perceive an object, already you are using two mental processes, which cannot in fact be separated, or exist the one without the other. In the first place there is simple awareness of a reality. You objectify an impression without arguing as to its reality at all, or relating it to yourself or anything else. You merely characterise the thing, and are aware of it as concrete and individual. This is the Pure Intuition. It has no admixture of intellectual process. And its salient characteristic is *that it is made or expressed by the mind,* and is indeed identical with this expression. You cannot separate the intuition from its expression. Moreover it is aesthetic in nature. Its character is identical with the character of the mind-process which makes the vision of the artist and the poet.

But this intuition is at once generalised, and related. The process of generalisation is the formation of the Concept, and is characteristic of the logical or intellectual activity. Moreover the Pure Concept is universal, and expressive, belonging to all individuals; concrete, and therefore real. Pseudo-concepts, which fail either in universality, expressiveness or concreteness, do exist and are of great value, but this value belongs not to the theoretical, but to the practical, activity. 'Evolution' is a pure concept, 'chair' a pseudo-concept. For our purpose it is not necessary to elaborate this point.

What does interest us is the relation between the two theoretical activities of the spirit—Intuition and Concept. They are 'moments in the unity of a single process.' Neither takes a prior place. "We cannot think without universalising, and we cannot have an intuition without thinking[6]." In other words, they are related in a synthesis that is *a priori*. This means that the intellectual activity which relates and generalises the intuitions or presentations does not depend upon them, but is as much a condition of experience as are the presentations themselves. Each of the two things, the intuition and the concept, is essential to knowledge; the concept is empty of content without the intuition, but you cannot have an intuition without thinking it. The two form an indivisible, organic unity; neither able to exist without the other. You cannot think without universalising, nor intuit without thinking. This is the logical *a priori* synthesis discovered by Kant. But Croce proceeds to use it in a wider sense, as we shall see.

These two elements then, the intuitional and the conceptual, together constitute the whole theoretic activity of knowing.

Now the first of these elements, the intuition, is expression of a reality to the self. It is essentially aesthetic, for aesthetic is the science of expressive activity. In forming an intuition, and expressing it, we compass Beauty, for Beauty is expression.

But there is another side to the activity of the spirit. Thinking and doing, willing and acting, go hand in hand.

The Practical Activity begins as Economic, directed towards particular ends. There is individual action; but there is also action universalised: directed to general ends: and this action is Ethical. Utility passes over into goodness: there is no good action which is not in some way useful, there is no useful action which is not in some way good.

Here again, then, we have two inseparable activities, related, as are the theoretic activities, as a first and second degree, yet each involving the other. The relation is identical with that of the *a priori* synthesis, and the term may be extended to cover this relation also.

Finally, the two sides of the activity of the spirit, the theoretic and the practical, are themselves related in this same double degree by a relation of synthesis that we may again term *a priori*. The theoretic activity cannot exist apart from the practical, nor the practical apart from the theoretic. The relation is again the same as that which obtains for the relation of the elements constituting each pair of the

[6] Wildon Carr, *The Philosophy of Croce*, p. 97.

four 'moments,' and for the pairs themselves. The *a priori* synthesis is extended to cover all these relations.

With Croce's theory of Beauty we have already made acquaintance. As we have seen, Kant laid the foundations by his discussion of the judgment of taste; Vico, by distinguishing the imaginative from the intellectual plane, had supplied the basal idea; but it was left to Croce to see that Beauty is expression, or the form given by the spirit to its intuitions, through which it makes contact with Reality. It must, however, be borne in mind that Croce draws an absolutely definite line between the expression, which belongs to the Theoretic Activity, and the technical embodiment of that expression, which belongs to the domain of the Practical. The work of art affords simply the stimulus which enables us to recreate the artist's expression; and it is the expression, not the work of art, that is beautiful. The Beautiful is a distinct concept; the Ugly is ugly in so far as it fails in distinctness, through failure to express. Beauty is simply aesthetic value—the value of the expressed intuition; ugliness the lack of aesthetic value, through lack of clarity in intuition and expression.

It is needless for us to follow out the rest of Croce's system. The chief point that remains is his identification of Philosophy with History—the *thought* about the presentation of Reality (Philosophy) with that presentation itself as an unfolding of immanent life (History). This identification really follows from the relation of the double degree between the theoretic and the practical. In thinking past history you bring it into the present as a practical issue; and you introduce the logical element in thinking it, but you could not do so if there were not an intuitive element in it intrinsically. Philosophy is historically conditioned; without philosophy there could be no history. With this line of argument, whose affinities with the philosophy of Bergson are obvious, Croce rounds off his system, completing his demonstration that the only Reality is living Spirit, immanent and unfolding.

Thus, according to Croce, the expressive nature of the Intuition, as it objectifies itself, and so differentiates itself from mere sensation, is appreciated by the mind, and serves as the first step in the formation of the Concept or judgment of definition. For the Concept is expressive, universal, and concrete. Through the Concept we arrive at knowledge of Reality; and this Concept reacts upon the Intuition, giving rise to the individual judgment. Croce shows, by demonstrating that analysis apart from synthesis, and equally synthesis apart from analysis, in any act of thought, is inconceivable, that one must, by an extension of the logical *a priori* synthesis, identify the judgment of definition and the individual judgment. You cannot, like the idealists, separate the concept from the facts, nor, like the empiricists, the facts from the concept. But neither in the realm of aesthetic interest can you separate the fact from its expressive intuition, or *vice versa*. The whole of Croce's system is, as he says, a philosophy of the spirit, which is itself all Reality. The activity of the spirit is twofold. In its theoretic activity there are two stages, Aesthetic and Logic, each involving the other, yet the first in a sense independent because primary, the second dependent on the first. In its practical activity there are also two degrees, the Economic and the Ethic, related to each other in the same way. Yet of these two activities, theoretic and practical, each involves the other, and in an *a priori* synthesis each substantiates the other.

It is not our purpose to examine the philosophy of Croce as a whole. Some points of disagreement with him will become manifest as we proceed to develop our discussion of the nature of beauty. Notably, we shall disagree with his rejection of a metaphysic and his denial of a God; since their inclusion is not really so inimical to his system as he supposes, their rejection by him would seem to be in a measure an accident of his circumstances, while their omission leaves the why? of spiritual and personal being unanswered. For the moment all we need is his discovery that Beauty is Expression, Aesthetic the Science of Expression; that to appreciate a work of art is to create it yourself by entering into the mind, and following the same path, as the original creator of it; and, first and most important of all, that our knowledge of the Real owes its possibility and its first beginnings to the movement of aesthetic intuition. It is a far cry from Plato to Croce.

If the fine arts be utterly distinct, having nothing in common save a background of emotion, this Essay is a meaningless attempt to express something which does not exist. It stands condemned; and this condemnation it shares with many nobler works. But if, as Croce urges, each art aims at presenting, through the practise of its own conventions, aspects of Truth which are suitable to that special medium, no effort to find a highest common factor of all arts is necessarily doomed to failure.

PART I:
THE THEORY.

What is Beauty? Many have asked it, and could find no answer because they understood their question no more than jesting Pilate understood his 'What is Truth?' But many beside have asked it with at least a real desire to understand. It was already in the mind of the prehistoric artist who was the first to draw a pattern or to sketch the mammoth, though no doubt he did not put the question to himself. It has been there, expressed or unexpressed, wherever a man has had vision enough to find his spirit stirred by a flower or a cathedral; a fabric or the low October sun upon a sheet of gossamer; wherever a man has tried to reproduce nature on canvas or pour out his longing and triumph in sound or written words. He has cried out that beauty dwells only in his own spirit, for there have been moods and days when he could see no beauty in that which at other times moved him deeply. Yet the agreement of civilised mankind, at all events, that this or that particular is beautiful is so widely diffused that he cannot but admit that something in the object itself must suggest the idea of beauty. Taste may change, but the sunset and the rose are universally acclaimed by all who have any aesthetic perception at all. On the other hand, faced with the vagaries of artistic fashion a man finds no absolute beauty, and is driven to a subjective theory, for he cannot admire the protruding, distorted lip so persuasive to certain savages. But no sooner is this theory constructed than he is brought up once more against the difficulty that an object is required before the sense of beauty is aroused, and that men do agree in attributing beauty to many things.

Because the perception of beauty involves a judgment (which really belongs to the intellectual process, and not properly to the aesthetic), beauty itself seems too elusive for definition. It has been left, as we have said, for Croce to formulate the first satisfactory concept of beauty. He saw what no one else had seen—that man's first contact with the Real, the first movement of the spirit that stretched beyond a mere sensation, was a creative act, an intuition not a judgment, expressing the reality to himself. Beauty, says Croce, is expression. Afterwards the man might give his expression objective form through some technique. Hence derive pictures, sculpture, music, dancing, poetry, drama, architecture, language itself; all the arts. Or the expression of his intuition may remain simply as a formative agent of his spirit. There are many mute inglorious Miltons. But he has expressed his intuition to himself, and it has formed a new material for his conceptual activity, whether or no he brings it far into the domain of the practical, through technique, in order that it may subserve some economic or moral function for himself and other men. That he must bring it into the practical in some measure, whether he does or does not give it technical form, is clear to anyone who has grasped Croce's main thought. The aesthetic intuition is for the individual, but he is driven to universalise it by thought (*i.e.* logic). It is of practical value to himself (economic motive) and it is capable of being made of use to others (ethical motive). Theoretic and practical cannot be isolated from one another.

As aesthetic is to logic, so is economic to ethic, and so is theoretic to practical; it is the relation of the double degree.

A priori synthesis unites each of the theoretic and of the practical activities with the other, and the same *a priori* synthesis unites the theoretic and the practical themselves, of which neither exclusively precedes the other in the circle of Real Being. This *is* the life of the spirit.

Now in considering this theory of Croce's we notice at once that mind or spirit is for him a datum, and that he assumes further that spirit is active and is definable only by its activity. He gives no reason for this activity. The cause of this is not far to seek, for his whole system is confessedly anti-metaphysical, and so, of necessity, stops short of ultimate things. Life, spirit, is for him the true mystery, and this is immanent. There is no room for transcendence. All he can say is that no philosophical system is definite because Life itself is never definite[7].

> Truth is always surrounded with mystery, an ascending to ever higher heights, which are without a summit, as Life is without a summit[8].

> The spirit,which is infinite possibility passing into infinite actuality, has drawn and draws at every moment the cosmos from chaos, has collected diffused life into the concentrated life of the organ, has achieved the passage from animal to human life, has created and creates modes of life ever more lofty. The work of the spirit is not finished and never will be finished. Our yearning for something higher is not vain. The very yearning, the infinity of our desire, is proof of the infinity of that process. The plant dreams of the animal, the animal of man, man of superman; for this, too, is a reality, if it be reality that with every historical movement man surpasses himself. The time will come when the great deeds and the great works now our memory and our boast will be forgotten, as we have forgotten the works and the deeds, no less great, of those beings of supreme genius who created what we call human life and seem to us now to have been savages of the lowest grade, almost men-monkeys. They will be forgotten for the document of progress is in *forgetting*; that is, in the fact being entirely absorbed in the new fact, in which, and not in itself, it has value. But we cannot know what the future states of Reality

---

[7] The clearest summary of Croce's position is to be found in the brief third section of the first part of his *Philosophy of the Practical*. Prof. Wildon Carr also has given a very clear account of Croce's philosophy as a whole in his book on *The Philosophy of Benedetto Croce*.

[8] *Philosophy of the Practical*, p. 591.

will be, in their determined physiognomy and succession, owing to the 'dignity' established in the Philosophy of the Practical, by which the knowledge of the action and of the deed follows and does not precede the action and the deed. *Mystery* is just the *infinity of evolution*; were this not so, that concept would not arise in the mind of man, nor would it be possible to abuse it, as it has been abused by being transported out of its place, that is to say, into the consciousness of itself, which the spiritual activity should have and has to the fullest degree, that is, the consciousness of its eternal categories.

The neglect of the moment of mystery is the true reason of the error known as the *Philosophy of History*, which undertakes to portray the plan of Providence and to determine the formula of progress. In this attempt (when it does not affirm mere philosophemes, as has very often happened), it makes the effort to enclose the infinite in the finite and capriciously to decree concluded that evolution which the universal spirit itself cannot conclude, for it would thus come to deny itself. In logic that error has been gnoseologically defined as the pretension of treating the individual as though it were the universal, making the universal individual; here it is to be defined in other words as the pretension of treating the finite as though it were the infinite, of making the infinite finite.

But the unjustified transportation of the concept of mystery from history, where it indicates the future that the past prepares and does not know, into philosophy, causes to be pointed as mysteries which give rise to probabilities and conjectures, problems that consist of philosophical terms, and should therefore be philosophically solved. But if the infinite progress and the infinite perfectibility of man is to be affirmed, although we do not know the concrete forms that progress and perfectibility will assume (not knowing them, because now it imports not to *know*, but to *do* them), then there is no meaning in positing as a mystery the immortality of the individual soul, or the existence of God; for these are not *facts* that may or may not happen sooner or later, but *concepts* that must be proved to be in themselves thinkable and not contradictory. Their thinkability will indeed be a mystery, but of the kind that it is a duty to make clear, because synonymous with obscurity or mental confusion. What has so far been demonstrated has been their unthinkability in the traditional form. Nor is it true that they correspond to profound demands of the human soul. Man does not seek a god external to himself and almost a despot, who commands and benefits him capriciously, nor does he aspire to an immortality of insipid ease; but he seeks for that God which he has in himself, and aspires to that activity which is both Life and Death[9].

Thus Croce affirms that evolution, development, is demanded by the very nature of spirit. In spirit the problem of the one and the many is solved. The yearnings of man towards something higher, and towards a unity that shall lie behind and stabilise all thought, are but expressions of the nature of Life. The dissatisfaction of such a thought is due to psychological illusion, comparable to a "dream of an art so sublime that every work of art really existing would by comparison appear contemptible." There is no intuition that cannot be clearly expressed; vague dreams of the Madonna of the Future end inevitably in an empty canvas. So too, according to Croce, is a dream of transcendence empty of content, because inexpressible; based on no clear intuition, but on a confusion between the historical judgment and some vague conception of the transcendental. And thus the life of the spirit is left a mystery.

We will not attempt any discussion of Croce's fundamental pantheism, neither will we as yet criticise his definition of Beauty. Instead, we will begin our constructive work by considering the psychological accompaniment of a perception of beauty and from that starting-point try to reach a conception and a definition that will carry us beyond Croce's into a region less empty of love, a region that shines with a light of its own. Dead moons are lovely, but they owe their loveliness to living light. Cold philosophies too are only beautiful when a beautiful spirit makes them seem to live.

Let us, then, turn to the psychological effects of that which appeals as beautiful to some individual mind, leaving on one side, for the time, all consideration of the reason why a particular object should rouse a sense of beauty in a particular mind.

Now unquestionably the beauty we perceive is never satisfying, or if it satisfies at all it does so but for a moment. Almost at once dissatisfaction follows, or rather unsatisfaction.

There is a yearning for something, a sense of something lacking. It is vague—so vague that the only representation of it that has ever adequately expressed at once its aspirations, its lack and its indeterminateness, is Blake's drawing "I want—I want." Of these three things it is compounded, of lack, of aspiration, and of self-ignorance that knows neither what it lacks nor what it desires; and these three determine its salient character—that of an impulse. That it is really an impulse becomes clear directly we examine its effects. It produces a desire to create. In the young, the uncontrolled, the illiterate, the creative impulse may be definitely sexual. Passion is undoubtedly stimulated in simple natures by the beautiful, and we shall see when we come to discuss the evolution of aesthetic sensibility that this fact is of the profoundest spiritual import. For the moment we need only note that this sex-impulse is creative. In natures artistically more developed yet not truly originative, the creative impulse is a desire to repeat the thing that has given this sense of beauty—to paint the sunset, to play the sonata, to declaim the poem. Yet even here we must note the germ of originality. The repetition is no mere reproduction. Elimination and emphasis make it in some measure a new

[9] *Philosophy of the Practical*, pp. 258-261.

creation. This is obvious in the less rigid arts, painting and music; but it is present even where the form is definite. Hear two different people, or the same person in two different moods, read the same poem, and see how different a thing it can be! In more artistic natures still, truly original, the desire to create is conscious, the desire to reproduce less. The thing created need not, probably will not, be of the same kind. The moon-glade on the sea enriching by contrast the blackness of the rocky headland, will inspire the musician to write, not a moonlight sonata, for true music is free from sensuous symbolism, but a pure rhythm of sound. To suggest visual symbols in sound is to prostitute music, to drive it back into the sensationalism from which it has freed itself. It is, further, to confuse the mind by attempting to combine two incompatible media of technical expression. As animal passion is to love, so is Carrier's "La Chasse" to a Bach prelude[10].

We see, then, that the psychological effect of the beautiful is to produce a creative impulse, based on the lack and the aspiration which give rise to a sense of yearning desire. We see that it is indeterminate, for it attempts to satisfy itself in very various ways. We see that in so far as it creates successfully, it finds some satisfaction.

Now all this fits admirably with Croce's theory of beauty. Beauty is for us the expression of that of which we have intuition. In realising the beauty of a symphony or picture we have ourselves re-created the intuition of the artist. In realising the beauty of a natural scene we have expressed an intuition of the reality that lies behind that scene; a creative act. We shall later go beyond Croce in this matter, referring our creative act to a re-creation of the intuition of God, and this will lead us to consider the aesthetic meaning of God's creation; but for the time we need not pursue this thought.

Our next business is, clearly, to analyse the yearning which precedes the creative act. We have said that this originates in dissatisfaction. What is this dissatisfaction? One other thing produces a feeling that is not merely analogous, but absolutely identical. When you love a person intensely and are uncertain if it is reciprocated, because no sign, or no sufficient sign, is given, you experience the same dissatisfaction, the same yearning and the same creative impulse. In primitive natures the impulse may fulfil itself in sexual excitement; in higher ones it is expressed in art. It is a commonplace to say that some of the world's greatest creative work is done under the stimulus of love. The poems of lovers furnish the most prominent example, not only their love poems, but the poems inspired by their love, like the *Divina Commedia*; but we need not seek far for examples in the other arts. Beethoven's Fourth Symphony was inspired by his love for the Countess Theresa von Brunswick. Tchaikovsky found inspiration in his Platonic love for Nadejda von Meck, whom he had never seen. His sad, abnormal friendships were an inspiration to Michael Angelo.

Now in both cases, paradoxical as it may seem, the dissatisfaction is due to receiving without giving. At first sight this seems to be exactly the opposite of the

---

[10] This is not to condemn programme music altogether, for much of the best programme music does not attempt to paint a scene in such a way as to call up visual images. *Vide infra.*

truth. Surely a man is pouring out his love, and receiving no return, one is inclined to say. But a moment's thought will convince us that the first statement is the true one. All the beauty, all the grace, all the interest and the charms of the loved one are given to us in unstinted measure, and we can give nothing in return. We may not even express our love, our desire to serve, but in the trivial services that convention allows. Yet how we prize these little services that we can render! How we seek out opportunity of rendering them! We receive; we can give no adequate return. It is that which determines our dissatisfaction. If the gift of our love is refused, dissatisfaction is most poignant. Commonly we say that the beloved refuses to give anything in such a case. Exactly the reverse is true. The beloved gives, and cannot avoid giving, but will receive nothing from us.

Now think of a perfect marriage or a perfect friendship. There is little trace of dissatisfaction there; only rest and happiness. We receive, but we give again, and our gift may be given without measure; may equal, or nearly equal what we receive; may at least be all that we can give. There is perfect reciprocity, and in reciprocity we find rest.

The creative impulse does not cease, service and gifts do not cease, but the spirit is free from longing dissatisfaction.

Turn now to the dissatisfaction produced by appreciation of the beautiful. We receive everything, we can give nothing at all (to the beautiful thing); and so dissatisfaction is at its highest. We love the thing in which we find beauty, but the love is one-sided. The cases are identical. It is no mere phrase when we speak of the love of beauty and the beauty of love. Unwittingly we express the truth of an absolute interdependence. *Love is relationship, beauty the expression of relationship.* In this sentence lies our thesis. Croce calls Beauty the expression of an Intuition; we shall define that intuition as the intuition of Relationship, Love being the relationship itself, intuitively known; known, that is, as Reality—as the fundamental quality of Personal Being, which is the only ultimate Reality. Because the intuition of Love is expressed, it enters immediately the domain of Aesthetic. Doubtless it is conceptualised; and hand in hand with this theoretic activity of the spirit goes the practical. Love is essentially practical, and, as Croce says, you can never separate or give priority to either the theoretic or the practical activity. The difference, then, between beauty and love that is returned lies in the fact that in the second there is reciprocity. You give, as well as receiving. In all love there is some reciprocity; the loved one cannot help being conscious of, and receiving, something of the spirit that moves out in such wise. The love of a being seen but once is purely aesthetic. Only this corresponds to the aesthetic appreciation of a scene, and even this not exactly; for the being is potentially capable of receiving, the scene is not.

It is worth noticing at this point that, though Greek thought arrived at no adequate idea of beauty, Greek Mythology did arrive at complete understanding. And this gives little cause for wonder, considering to what a level the love of the beautiful developed in ancient Greece, and considering too how myth represents the unreasoned, intuitive wishes and ideas of an infantile age[11]. We often wonder

[11] Cf. the work of the psychoanalytic school, especially Jung's *Psychology of the Unconscious* and Rivers' *Dreams and Primitive Culture.*

at the depths which mythology plumbs. Accepting Croce's scheme, it is the more easy to understand. The myth of Pygmalion is subtly suggestive. Pygmalion created beauty, and longed for it to reciprocate his love, and out of his longing life and love were born. Beauty was for him one-sided love; hence his yearning and his dissatisfaction.

But we are not Pygmalions. Our Galatea never comes to life. Why then should we strive still to create? Why like the man in the old play, should we proceed with an endless task: "When will you finish Campaspe?" "Never finish, for always in absolute beauty there is somewhat above art[12]." Croce simply takes activity as the character of spirit and leaves it at that, admitting, but not really explaining, the fact that men are dissatisfied with the mystery of it all. We, approaching with a different presupposition, accepting God and not rejecting metaphysic, may hope to find some fuller explanation. We do in fact go on creating something that cannot reciprocate. Why? First of all, by our creative act we learn more of the meaning of the Reality that is around us, and the Reality that is ourself. We find the creative godhead of our personality, we exercise our self in its true function of godhead. Moreover, we create a gift to other men, whether technically or otherwise. If we cannot give to nature, we can at least give our understanding of nature to our fellows:

> Better to sit at the water's birth
> Than a sea of waves to win,
> To live in the love that floweth forth
> Than the love that floweth in.
>
> Be thy heart a well of love, my child,
> Flowing, and free, and sure,
> For a cistern of love, though undefiled
> Keeps not the spirit pure[13].

And neither does the spirit that is a cistern of beauty fulfil itself, nor remain pure.

Our aesthetic activity is, then, our first contact with Reality, paving the way to an understanding of the meaning of that Reality. In spite of Croce, we cannot agree that a full appreciation of this meaning could be considered as achieved if the end is simply longing—dissatisfaction. In the very fact that beauty produces in us a yearning, that issues in a creative activity which does not, and cannot, satisfy the yearning, we have evidence that the solution is not found. In the identity of psychological content produced by beauty and by unrequited love we find the clue we seek. In the restfulness of a perfect friendship, of an intercourse which knows no subject that must not be touched upon, fears no jarring note, whatever matter comes upon the scene, can give all the keys in perfect trust, knowing that trust will never be regretted, and hold the other's keys knowing there is the same confidence on that side; that can see with the other's eyes, and never fear to be itself misunderstood; in that restfulness the problems of beauty, of life, of Reality itself find answer.

---

[12] Lyly's *Campaspe*.
[13] G. Macdonald, *Phantastes*.

Let us repeat. The unsatisfyingness of beauty is due to the fact that you are taking and not giving. In order to give *something*, to others, though not to the object that roused in you the sense of beauty, you create by some technique. What is it you are receiving? An intuition, which you express to yourself creatively and to others through its effect on your character;—to which further, if you are an artist, you give external, technical expression. This intuition which you receive is the first stage of knowledge—of the knowledge of Reality. So far, agreeing with Croce, we agree with Bergson; and moreover we leave room for mysticism, since mysticism becomes the appreciation of relationship, and logic paves the way for suitable activity to develop our side of the relationship. The meaning of this becomes clearer when we consider Croce's explanation of the process of perceiving beauty in the work of an artist, be it picture, symphony, or poem. He points out that in appreciating a work of art you enter into the mind of the creator, follow his intuition, and create the expression afresh for yourself. On the degree in which you can do this depends the fullness of your appreciation of the work.

But when you see beauty in a natural object the matter is less clear. Croce would say that you are in the first stage of knowing that object, and he is unquestionably right so far. But can we not, using the analogy of the picture or the poem, go on to say that you are following out the idea of the creator of the natural object—that you are in touch with the Cosmic Idea, which is the Idea of a Personal God? If so, there is indeed room for mysticism, for mysticism becomes simply the realisation that you are in fact doing this. Moreover, Beauty and Love at once fall into relation. Beauty is not simply expression, but the expression of a relation, and it is incomplete because the relation is not yet reciprocal. Love is that relation itself.

In another aspect, beauty is seen as the meeting-place for love, since it is the expression of an intuition of Reality, and Reality is rooted and grounded in love. Where there is limitation either of one or both of two persons, expression is needed to provide a meeting-place—speech or sign for the lesser artist, music, poetry, or picture for the greater. Each expression is a symbol of the reality it incarnates; in so far as it reaches out beyond its own immediate apprehension of that reality. All expression, all art, is symbolic and has a mystical aspect, else it would be either complete and all-embracing or devoid of real content. So far the symbolists are right.

But this opens up a wide problem. If Beauty be the formulated intuition of Reality, which, because of its incompleteness, represents in symbols things that are beyond its immediate purview, and if Reality be, as we have elsewhere argued[14], grounded on Personal Relationship, the self-expression of Love, does beauty cease when personal relations become perfect? For we have argued that a symbol belongs to the domain of the imperfect, not the perfect[15]. If so, has beauty any meaning for God? At this point we clearly come into contact with the problem of God's creative activity. We have said[16] that the creation of God must be the creation of something new. We have said that Love, of its own nature, demands expansion, is

---

[14] *Evolution and Spiritual Life* and *Evolution and the Doctrine of the Trinity.*

[15] *Evolution and Spiritual Life.*

[16] *Opp. citt. passim.*

centrifugal as well as centripetal, and in this centrifugality of love we sought the Divine Impulse to create new personalities. But behind lurked always the question "How could a God whose experience was perfect and embraced already all Reality, create anything that was new?" The reciprocity of perfected love would be new for the personal beings He had created; but His self-limitation which the freedom of those beings necessitated would not be new for Him, for self-abnegation is an eternal part of love, since love is substantiated as itself by creative self-surrender, transcendence by immanence. Would the *result* of His self-limitation be new for Him, implicit as it is in His Being as Love? Would the experience of the reciprocal love of His children be a new thing for Him?

No doubt the problem, as belonging to the domain of the Transcendent, is not soluble for us, whose transcendence, whose intuition of the Real, is so incomplete. But because in such measure as we do know the Real we are ourselves transcendent, we can at least hope to touch the fringe of His garment; and Croce's proof that pure intuition — which Bergson also urges to be our *point d'appui* with the Real — belongs to the domain of aesthetic, gives us a fresh clue in our investigation.

Beauty is expression. This is Croce's statement; and in it we find what we need, provided that we expand the definition into 'the expression of Relation.' If there be a Personal God as we believe, whose experience is Reality, He must always be expressing that Reality. There is no consciousness without expression. But the expression of knowledge of the Real is Beauty. God's Being must be full of an overwhelming Beauty. But part of His Nature, as Love, is centrifugal. That centrifugal part must also be expressed. The artist follows his expression by technical application; he paints for eye or ear, to satisfy himself and to communicate his intuition. In so far as he fails in his expression, the result is ugly. In so far, also, as God's creation fails, through its own inevitable condition of the freedom of man, the result is ugly. Ugliness is the aesthetic, or theoretical aspect of sin; in its practical aspect sin is uneconomic, un-moral.

Now if one thing is more certain than another, it is that Beauty is for ever new. Each sense of beauty is a new creation, a fresh activity of the spirit, be it inspired never so often by the same object. And this means that to know the Real is for ever a new thing. God's love is always new for Himself. His self-knowledge is creation perpetually renewed. It follows, *a fortiori*, that His knowledge of the beings He creates and is creating is each moment new. Because knowledge is in its first movement Beauty, there can be no stagnancy in Eternal Being, no dead level of satiety in Eternal Life.

Beauty is expression. For God it is the expression of His relation to Himself as transcendent, and of the substantiation of His transcendence through His relation to others as immanent, in the first stage of the movement of that relation towards and into transcendence. Beauty is the expression of a relation, and is ever new. But the relation itself is Love. God is Love; that love is expressed as Beauty; and Beauty is necessarily eternal, because it is the knowledge of Reality. God is Love. This is to say that God IS because He is a relation, to Himself and to others. Here is the inmost heart of Trinitarian Doctrine, as we have seen[17]. Because He is Love, He

[17] *Evolution and the Doctrine of the Trinity.*

expresses that Reality in activity. But activity has two sides, the theoretical and the practical. His expression is, on the theoretic side, Beauty, and is hence for ever new for Him. He is for Himself a Relation, known intuitively and expressed as Beauty, and His intuition of this Reality is ever new. On the practical side it is Creation, full of purpose (economic aspect) and of goodness (moral aspect); new for us, His creatures, but only achieving, for us even, its full newness as we come to know the Reality which is the experience of the Love that is perfect in Him alone; only achieving its full newness as we begin ourselves to know, to express, and to create: as we become gods ourselves. And what He creates is real, beautiful, and new.

Beauty is eternal. It is the meeting-place of personal beings for ever; but it is a symbol only so long as these personal beings are imperfect, and their knowledge incomplete. Beauty and knowledge become coextensive as immediate intuition extends its boundaries till logic has no more a place, or rather till logic and intuition cover the same ground. So too with the practical; the useful extends its boundaries till it is coextensive with the good, and the two become one and the same. The activity that remains is as God's activity. Love is itself because it is both knowing and doing; absolute Being is the circle of these two inseparables.

Before we proceed it will be as well to remind ourselves once more of the psychological fact that has caused us to modify Croce's definition of beauty by introducing the idea of relation. This characteristic consequence of a vision of the beautiful is the sense of longing, akin to the longing of unreciprocated love, which issues in some creative act. This act may be a conscious attempt to produce something of aesthetic value—a work of art—or it may simply be an attempt to make our *milieu* harmonious. The housewife may be stimulated to re-cover the cushions, to tidy the house, or to re-arrange the room; the mother may try to make her children happier; the selfish man or the fractious child may try to make life more complete and harmonious by loving deeds, however short-lived. The most commonplace mind may feel a religious impulse; a sense of wonder and reverence. Men have always been perplexed by the apparently close connection between the beautiful and the good, between the beautiful and the sublime. This connection becomes clear in the light of our definition. Beauty is seen as the first step towards an understanding of Reality, and that Reality is Love, personal relationship, reciprocity. Relationship between finite persons first (yet not transient even here, because personality is essentially infinite, and persons are only limited in so far as they have failed as yet to achieve personality), but relationship that finds its origin and explanation in the personal, creative, Triune Being of God[18]. The perception of beauty is accompaniedby emotion; free, as emotion is in itself, though aroused by external conditioning[19]; yet unsatisfied, thwarted, and so with a vein of sadness in its joy. Its joy is the joy of beginning to understand. All understanding is pleasure. One smiled with pleasure when one first grasped Euclid's forty-seventh proposition, even. But here we understand the beauty as a symbol and a meeting-place. It makes us feel less lonely and less isolated. Its sadness is the sadness of

[18] I make no apology for not entering here on any discussion of how God can be Love. I have endeavoured to offer suggestions on this matter in my earlier books, and especially in *Evolution and the Doctrine of the Trinity*.

[19] *Evolution and the Doctrine of the Trinity*, ch. III.

an incomplete understanding. We see in a beautiful thing a thing that can receive nothing from us, while it gives much to us. Yet the very fact that beauty does make us 'feel religious' shows that somehow we do realise that we can give something to God, and find a little satisfaction in doing so; that even nature is not so impersonal as we were inclined to think. Our desire to create beautiful things is a sign that we understand our self also, our destined godhead, and that we too wish to reveal our self by creating for others, and giving to others. It is a sign that we understand that our relations with God and with our fellows are reciprocal.

Croce gives the clue when he shows that aesthetic is the first stage of the spirit's activity. Bergson strikes a note that wakes an answering harmony when he urges that intuition brings us nearer to Reality than does intellect directed toward practical aims, even though some of his deductions displease; Kant and Hegel indicate the eternal value of aesthetic when they urge that it belongs to the highest and last stage. But Croce gives no reason for the longing that beauty forces upon us; nor indeed for the activity of spirit at all; he merely assumes spirit as a datum, and is defined by its activity.

But if we regard beauty as the expression of a perceived relationship, almost as one-sided love, the whole falls into place. Through beauty we get into touch with Reality, which Reality is, in its completeness, the mutual activity of Love. The basis of Love's activity is Love's freedom, even its freedom to limit itself. Mankind is winning freedom out of determined conditions; which conditions are the creation, the expression, of God's love, through self-limitation. Because they are the expression of God's knowledge of the Reality of Love, they are beautiful. The winning of freedom by man is achieved through adaptative relation to the environment. As this adaptation becomes conscious—as we gain intuitive knowledge of the environment—the sense of beauty is born, for we express our knowledge of this relation to ourselves; and make efforts towards further adaptation. These efforts are creative; and as we progress our creation becomes more and more altruistic; a creation for others with our relationship to them held consciously before us. These few words will suffice to show how perfectly our thesis fits in with the evolutionary views we have previously enunciated. The development of this side of the argument may be left for the present.

One other matter requires a brief consideration, and then we can leave the general outline of our theory and proceed to a more detailed treatment of certain parts of it. This is the old, unsolved problem whether beauty is subjective or objective; whether a thing is beautiful in itself, or whether it is only our thinking that makes it so. Croce has made it perfectly clear that the thing or the scene which we erroneously call beautiful, meaning that it is beautiful in itself, physically beautiful, is simply the "stimulus to aesthetic reproduction, which presupposes previous production. Without preceding aesthetic intuitions of the imagination, nature cannot arouse any at all." Perhaps Croce's own thesis would gain in clearness and coherence if, starting from the sense of beauty aroused by a work of art as the re-creation of the artist's intuition by the spectator, he had accepted the religious implication, and argued that appreciation of so-called natural beauty, was the re-creation by man of God's intuition. But, with his prejudice against religion, he naturally could not boldly accept God as the Primal Artist, even though to do so would have made his theory far more complete, and would have saved him from relegating the chief factor of man's life to the realm of psychological illusion.

To return to the immediate question, there can, of course, be no doubt that since beauty is an activity of the spirit, the expression of an intuition, beauty itself must be purely subjective. Equally, there can be no doubt that without the objective Reality the intuition could never be called into being. (We call it definitely objective for man, since all our argument in previous works has driven us to the conclusion that there is a necessary dualism for man as long as freedom is incomplete, love imperfect; as long, that is, as man is becoming.)

This grows more and more clear as one analyses the things that have roused in oneself the keenest sense of beauty. I think of a copse starred with snowdrops and aconite amid bare trunks under a steel-grey sky—a day in late autumn in water-meadows; emerald peacock-tails of weed in the river, and lights of madder and old gold—blue sea covered with pearly Portuguese men-o'-war and white surf breaking on black lava rocks—perhaps a dozen such landmarks, to me a priceless possession, to another about as interesting as an album of picture-postcards from somebody else's travels. In mercy partly, partly in self-defence, one withholds these things from all but the few who care to understand. Let each fill in his own; for there are in every life such moments, when one is in touch with a larger life, and it is these moments which make a man, as Masefield has wonderfully shown in his poem *Biography*. Then there are the hours when human triumphs rouse in us the same ecstasy. Bach preludes and fugues, with their palaces reared by perfect stone added architecturally to perfect stone; the dainty certainties of Mozart; the sad gaiety and foreboding meditations of Chopin; the delicate cadences of Swinburne; the lusty, open-air searchings of Masefield, saddened by the obsession of sunset transience; the gentle longing of the refrain of the *Earthly Paradise*; the massive synthesis of the *Dynasts*; the sorrow of *Deirdre* and *Violaine*; the ethereal atmosphere of *A Midsummer Night's Dream*; pictures—architecture—it is all endless. Now the first thing we notice is that if we are in the wrong mood these things may have little or no appeal. I may walk in Water-meads and feel nothing of their charm. Bach may be mere noise, if I want to think of something else. Again the Madonna of the Magnificat may leave me unmoved, if my attention is on other matters. Those whose sense of beauty is really keen can never be unstirred by the beautiful, unless their attention is so rivetted on other things that they do not observe it at all, but most of us are of commoner clay; we can notice a thing yet hardly be aware of its beauty.

Here, in either case, our ordinary speech hits the nail exactly on the head: "I am not in a receptive mood," we say. I do not receive what these things have to give. In an appreciative mood I take something from the thing that seems to me beautiful—this act is my intuition—and use it as the basis of my creative work— my expression. I need the presentation of an external object, or its memory, for that creation. Now, as we have just seen, a host of very different objects excite in an individual emotion of beauty in a pre-eminent degree, while if we reckon the objects which excite it in a less acute form, the tale is endless; yet the emotion all excite is sufficiently the same in content, in spite of its multiplicity of form, to be expressed by the single term beauty. One is tempted to speak loosely of this effect of the beautiful on us as an emotion, though clearly it is not one, since it is expression. An emotion may be beautiful immediately it is known and expressed in this act of knowing, but the emotion is not beautiful any more than any other object is beautiful. Nevertheless, this loose usage of the term has one advantage. It draws our attention to the close relationship that binds together beauty and emotion. We have seen elsewhere that in the realm of emotion exists the freedom that lies between the incoming perception and the outgoing activity, forming the bond between the first and last, and determining the form of the response to the stimulus[20]. In the recognition of beauty there is freedom and emotion, as there is in every creative act. But the activity is dependent on stimulus, and every stimulus is primarily perceptual, though not necessarily in the strict sense of being perceived by an organ of sense. The perception may be wholly internal, the self being its own object in introspection[21]; the intuition may be the intuition of love itself. Here we see the origin of the common, yet I believe erroneous, statement that "beauty, as we understand it, is only for sense and for sensuous imagination[22]." If Beauty be the expression of an intuition of Reality, as Croce says, and Reality be ultimately the activity of Personal Being, which activity is relationship, as we have seen reason to claim[23], Beauty is not dependent on sense perception alone. Further, because the activity of personal relation is Love, we see in Beauty the creative knowledge of love, which is necessarily linked in closest intimacy with freedom and emotion. Love is not beautiful; it is simply the activity of relationship. The knowledge of love is Beauty's very self. The world is not beautiful, but knowledge of the world as the expression of a part of Reality—of that portion of Reality which is limited and determined by the self-abnegation of God's love—is Beauty. In so far as we merely perceive matter the aesthetic side is in abeyance. At this moment we know, not Reality, but Appearance. Our unaesthetic moods are determined by our more or less complete practical concern with Appearance, our more or less complete blindness to Reality. We have gone back to a lower, more primitive stage. In our limited and still largely determined existence we are bound to be occupied in a great measure with appearance. The practical must dominate the theoretic activity; the spirit must be unbalanced, asymmetrical. Even in our moments of greatest symmetry our apprehension of the Real is largely at second hand. *Pace*, Croce, we would say—as we have said already[24]—that the Immanent cannot have immediate contact with the Real; man's intuitions belong to his transcendence where they deal with the absolutely Real. Man immanent and limited is immediately in contact with God immanent and self-limited; only in so far as man is transcendent is he in contact with God Transcendent, and so in touch with the Whole. In his immanence man lives by symbols, which are sacraments; and here we find the symbolic aspect of Beauty. It is the material basis of this symbolic side of Beauty, rather than Beauty absolute, that has of necessity received most attention hitherto; and the puzzles of rival theories have arisen through failure to

[20] *Evolution and the Doctrine of the Trinity*, ch. III.

[21] *Ibid*. See also Strong, *The Origin of Consciousness*.

[22] Bosanquet, *History of Aesthetic*, p. 37.

[23] McDowall, *opp. citt*.

[24] *Evolution and Spiritual Life*.

realise that a symbol is a partial expression of a reality, and that it can only be fully grasped when the reality which it symbolises is understood. A symbol has something of the reality itself, or it would not be a symbol, but it does not represent that reality adequately, or it would be co-extensive with it; would *be* the reality itself. Beauty is thus subjective, in so far as it is necessarily the work of the spirit. But it is objective in so far as the reality of which it is the knowledge is personal and external to the self, and will always remain external, however complete the interpenetration of personalities, since personalities cannot be merged and lost in each other, but remain eternally in their self-identity[25].

A natural object *per se* is not beautiful; only so far as it is understood as a partial representation of Reality, a symbol, is it beautiful.

Naturally, this statement arouses the objection that to most people the music of Grieg, if not of Bach, the pictures of Leighton, if not of Utamaro, are beautiful; and that there is a general consensus of opinion that the view over the Severn from the Windcliff, or the view of Lisbon from the harbour is more beautiful than Wormwood Scrubbs. The answer to the first part of this objection is obvious. In music, painting, verse, we are re-creating for ourselves the artist's intuition. We know that he found beauty, and he has abstracted in his art in such a way as to render the beauty more easily recaptured. The artist is then our guide. He was an artist because his spirit was more sensitive to the reality than ours, and we follow him.

But in natural beauty, too, is not this true? Primitive peoples who live amid the most lovely scenery have little or no perception of it. But there are places and scenes where nature seems to have performed a sort of process of abstraction for us. The elements are simplified and harmonious, and there is little to distract the attention from certain main features. A comparatively large number of people will have a sufficiently developed spirit to get into touch with something beyond the mere object at such places. More education in abstraction and intuition is required to perceive some kinds of beauty; we see the same thing even in the artistic creation of men. Mendelssohn appeals to far more than Bach; Leader to far more than Botticelli. Moreover, the more obvious kinds of natural beauty, as we may loosely term them, will appeal to many lesser artists, who will give technical expression to them. We shall be thus familiarised with these representations, through pianolas and art-magazines and penny readings, or through concerts and picture galleries and study; and shall be the more prepared to intuit for ourselves when we meet with objective elements of a somewhat similar type. And we have further argued that even in natural beauty we are really following the intuition of Creative Mind.

One other point is perhaps worthy of remark. Natural science appears to compass a very large achievement in knowledge, and to express this knowledge with singular felicity; yet in science there is little that can be called beautiful, except in a highly metaphorical sense. The explanation of this anomaly is clear and incontrovertible. The work of theoretical science is essentially abstract, and is concerned wholly with Appearance, not Reality, except where it impinges upon the domain

---

[25] *Evolution and Spiritual Life,* ch. VI, and *Evolution and the Doctrine of the Trinity,* ch. VI.

of philosophy. The intuition of Beauty is an intuition of Reality.

We may now put down our conclusions in a brief and more regular form:

(1) External things are required to rouse in me a sense of beauty, but they are not in themselves beautiful.

(2) I create their beauty, by understanding them as parts of a Whole which is Reality.

(3) Beauty is expression; I must therefore form a clear intuition and express it to myself. This is my creative act; to which I may, or may not, give a technical embodiment.

(4) But I am not merely creating a photographic image, an imitation. I am getting into a certain receptive condition in which I can abstract from what I see its essence and fit this into my knowledge of Reality. I cannot see a thing as beautiful unless in some degree it gives me this impression of relatedness to Reality and to myself—linking me with the Reality of which I am a part. Beauty thus comes to be a felt relationship. My creation is the creation of a fuller understanding of relatedness.

(5) I am always dissatisfied with Beauty, which wakes in me a sense of longing exactly the same as the longing of an unreciprocated love. I receive and cannot give. Yet in this beauty and this love there is joy as well as sorrow.

(6) My life is part of an organic Whole whose ultimate meaning and purpose is personal relationship—interpenetration. The dissatisfaction is due to a sense of imperfect interpenetration. What is needed, and is felt to be needed, is equal give and take—reciprocal creative activity. Dissatisfaction comes when giving and taking are not balanced.

(7) Beauty is eternal, since the creative expression of Love is eternal, and Love knows eternally what it is—is eternally self-conscious. Love is relation, beauty the expression of the immediate knowledge of that relation.

(8) This knowledge is always a new, creative act. God must continually express His Being as Love else He would cease to be Love and so to be at all. In Creative Expression He renews Himself. He is for Himself ever new. And, because Love is centrifugal as well as centripetal, He must for ever express Himself *outwards*, so to speak, in the creation of other beings, and this His work of self-abnegation is new and beautiful.

(9) We have hardly touched on the problem of the ugly. We have little to add to Croce's explanation of it as the failure of expression—as the failure to express coherent unity—which involves the failure of intuition. We shall just touch upon it hereafter; at the moment all we need do is to remind ourselves that the ugliest thing in the world is sin, because it is the failure to understand the whole, and to express the fullest, greatest beauty.

PART II:
BEAUTY IN EVOLUTION.

Theories of aesthetic, so far, have paid little attention to the development of the sense of beauty, except perhaps in the individual. This was natural enough so long as the idea of evolution was unformulated, or, if touched upon speculatively, played little part in men's general attitude to life; and since the doctrine of evolution came to its own, little original work, beyond that of Croce, has been done in this region. Croce touches the evolutionary aspect but lightly, though it is implicit in his identification of History with Philosophy:

> "Since all the characteristics assigned to Philosophy are verbal variants of its unique character, which is the pure concept, so all the characteristics of History can be reduced to the definition and identification of History with the individual judgment[26]." "If History is impossible without the logical, that is, the philosophical, element, philosophy is not possible without the intuitive, or historical element[27]." "Philosophy, then, is neither beyond, nor at the beginning, nor at the end of history, nor is it achieved in a moment or in any single moment of history. It is achieved *at every moment* and is always completely united to facts and conditioned by historical knowledge.—The *a priori* synthesis, which is the reality of the individual judgment and of the definition, is also the reality of philosophy and of history. It is the formula of thought which by constituting itself qualifies intuition and constitutes history. History does not precede philosophy, nor philosophy history; both are born at one birth[28]."

This view, however interesting and suggestive it may be in the realmof pure thought, for the simple reason that it does not boldly grapple with the fact of *practical* dualism, is difficult of application to the process of the dawn of consciousness. Croce's whole philosophy is directed to the denial of dualism; it is a new form of idealistic monism. We have been led in our earlier reasonings to deny an ultimate dualism[29], but we have also been led to affirm dualism as existent in Time, through the self-limitation and immanence of Eternal Spirit. On this basis, at which we arrived through a detailed consideration of the process of inorganic

[26] Croce, *Logic*, p. 279.
[27] *Ibid.* p. 310.
[28] Croce, *Logic*, pp. 324-325.
[29] McDowall, *opp. citt.*

and organic evolution, we reared our whole superstructure. On this same basis, then, we will attempt to reason out a view of the evolution of beauty that shall be in harmony both with the facts of evolution and with the theocentric system that issued from our discussion as apparently the only possible explanation of the universe, so far, at least, as its broad outline was concerned.

If beauty be the expression of an intuition, and if, further, the intuition required involves a sense of relation, there can be no true perception of beauty until self-consciousness arises. Broadly speaking, this is to say there can be no sense of beauty except in man.

But here at once we are brought up against the fact of sexual selection. Surely the posturings of spiders, the dance of the ruff, the display of the peacock and the Bird of Paradise, the song of the warbler (if indeed this be a courting and hymeneal song) do imply some aesthetic preference in the mate? Still more does the elaborate performance of the Bower-bird, with its love-chase through the gay parterres of its carefully decked garden and in and out of the double-doored bower, suggest some sense of beauty.

This fact, which at first sight seems fatal to our whole theory, really supplies us with the clue we lacked.

Perhaps, even at this moment of courting, there is no true self-consciousness. Our previous discussions have led us to question whether this exists at all in animals, except possibly in a few of those most developed through contact with man. But there is unquestionably a sense of relation. The male and female are urged to love-play by the sexual impulse, and this necessarily involves a sense of inter-relatedness. It may not be—probably is not—sufficiently conscious of the self and the other to be termed love. It is a mere sense of the necessity of the other for fulfilling a need as urgent and as little understood as hunger.

But in the sex-impulse we find a beginning of the fact of inter-relation; and this is the foundation we require. The elaborate instances we have mentioned go a step farther than the simple sex-need. There is a definite attempt to make that need reciprocal by stimulating the dormant sense of relation in the mate through the use of objects to which a *meaning* is given through emphasis or through arrangement and juxtaposition. And this meaning is recognised, though perhaps not as beauty exactly; that would imply the expression of the meaning to the self, and it is doubtful if the self yet exists. But it is very hard to draw any line. At all events we can say that here there is relation—and *self-conscious* relation is love; and that here is expression of a meaning and a need—and a *recognised* meaning, or intuition, when expressed to the self is beauty. We are on the confines of aesthetic. Now at first sight this idea may raise a feeling of antagonism, almost of disgust. We seem to have reduced beauty to terms of the sexual impulse. Further consideration will serve to dispel this sense of a derogation of beauty, and will even give to the sex-impulse itself a nobler significance, making it appear as the first stage in the emergence of Love and Beauty; rendering to it the honour due from an understanding of the end which it subserves. There can be little doubt that in man the perception of beauty in the opposite sex—not *as* beauty perhaps, but as simple attraction to a beautiful person—does very generally precede that of more impersonal forms of beauty. Amid savage races this is unquestionably the case. The strange decoration of the body and other rites in the initiation of the adolescent, are undoubtedly expressions connected with sex-relations. To us they are ugly because they fail to express our fuller understanding; to the savage they are beautiful. And I believe that in the children of a highly developed artistic race it is true also in some measure. The love-admiration of boys and girls begins at a very tender age; and the psychoanalytic work of Freud and Jung gives a significance, no doubt often exaggerated, to acts and thoughts and dreams of children which, if not strictly sexual in the common sense, are yet connected with the impulse— called by Jung the *libido*—that underlies the evolution of the race. If we employ the terminology of Bergson and Driesch, we may say that the *élan vital*, or *entelechy*, is the *libido* of Jung; that, as the animal progresses along the path of evolution, it becomes the sexual impulse in the wider sense given to the term by Freud; and that in one aspect it finally becomes the sexual impulse in the sense in which the term is commonly understood, while it achieves infinitely higher levels in the direction of spiritual progress at the same time. But observe what this implies. We have just noticed the obvious fact that the sex-impulse involves a sense of relation. It is probable that the first dawnings of relationship, albeit in a primitive, almost sensational form, arise here. The using of inanimate objects as tools is probably evolved later than conjugation, even in the protozoa. *Difflugia* may make use of grains of sand to form its test, but all protozoa conjugate. Anyhow, this is a minor matter. The important point is that in the sex-impulse arises first the sense of a relation between individuals, which is destined, far later, to grow into the first stages of love; and in the development of the child we find traces of this origin, distorted and chronologically misplaced, exactly as one would expect from the Law of Recapitulation.

Another point of interest arises here. Many psychoanalysts, and notably Jung[30], have shown that mythology has an overwhelmingly sexual content. Further, Rivers[31], and others, have extended the conception of the primitive, or infantile, character of myth in relation to the primitive or infantile character of dreams, showing that both belong to a lower level of culture than does the waking self. As time goes on more and more, not only of the minor activities of the individual, but of the earlier activities of the race, are relegated to the unconscious. Psychologists have long recognised this fact in dealing with habit-formation, but these recent writers have given it a deeper significance. The spirit uses the past as something on which to build the future. In old days, and among primitive peoples still to-day, the explanation of life was sought in a very childish manner. The impulse of sex was not understood, its relation to procreation was largely hidden, as witness the ceremonies of Intichiuma, and many others that, by symbolic magic, should confer fertility. It was mysterious, yet immensely powerful. It had some sort of relation to the birth of children and animals. The creation of all things was mysterious, but since the new was born these two mysteries must be connected. Hence the sexual symbolism of myths that were predominantly aetiological in character—that were predominantly attempts to answer the great Why? of the universe.

[30] *The Psychology of the Unconscious.*
[31] *Dreams and Primitive Culture.*

In the present connection, then, the chief interest of the work of Freud and Jung on infantile phenomena associated with sex, in so far as it is not exaggerated, lies in the fact that here too we have an instance of the working of von Baer's Law of Recapitulation. In the animal the sense of relation begins with sex; in the child we have strange, fragmentary primitive sex-phenomena (if these psychoanalysts be right), dissociated from many of their natural concomitants; phenomena suggesting some close analogy with the temporary appearance in the embryo of structures that disappear again, having lost their significance. Can it be that the purely animal basis on which man's great structure of relationship is raised, is merely a foundation, becoming gradually hidden, covered up?

Love is, no doubt, in origin an impulse of sex. Yet the highest love we know and experience in ourselves has nothing sexual in it. When a man and a maid fall in love there is no thought of such things in the mind of either. Primarily, true love is utterly pure from admixture with animal instincts, though it may be, and is, founded on them in the evolutionary sense, and though they still play a vastly important part, made beautiful by the love they subserve. But the love that *begins* as conscious sex-instinct is no love at all. There is love between men and women, even young men and women, as well as between those of the same sex, that is either utterly free from all sexual content, or in which that content is so trivial in amount, and so completely dismissed from attention, that it is practically non-existent. If one is conscious of it at any moment, one is so by a definite effort of the mind, and for the specific purpose of bringing before oneself the wonderful emergence of the purest and highest activity of the spirit from so lowly and physical an origin. Such love is far higher than the love between husband and wife often is, where the sexual side is primary as well as primitive, and friendship secondary. Only when husband and wife are first friends, and then, after that, live together with a full realisation of the sacramental meaning of sex as the foundation on which the eternal temple of love has been and is being built, can their union approach the highest level. Then it is indeed the best of all in this life. It takes them closer to the heart of things than mere friendship would, and enables them to make their other friendships perfect through the understanding which it brings. The physical subserves the spiritual, and even in the physical the two are united. The physical and the spiritual are for them one — parts of a whole. Their own friendship is perfect as far as anything human can be perfect, and by it their friendships with others are made perfect.

We see, then, in the founding and development of the sexual impulse the first movement of the *élan vital* along its true path of evolution. The *élan vital* determines progress; it is the unrest, the divine discontent of spirit creating itself in matter[32]. It progresses along various roads, but the road that leads it to its own fulfilment lies through sex. The *élan vital* becomes *libido* in an even narrower sense than that, almost co-extensive with Bergson's term, which Jung gives to the word. For through sex the sense of individual, and subsequently personal, inter-relationship comes into being[33]. With the arousing of self-consciousness we find the dawn

[32] For the exact sense in which these words are used, and for their implications in regard to God's creative activity, see *Evolution and the Need of Atonement*.

[33] A word may be said concerning the personal relationship of fear and hate. Here in

of love. This is the beginning of understanding. In the intuition of love is born the knowledge of Reality. Faint, partial, obscured by the sex-basis on which it is built up, it is yet the key to the mystery of being. Gradually, slowly, amid disappointing foulness and blind passion, it still grows. In its insistence on relationship it is manifested as the human aspect of religion. Side by side with it grows the knowledge and love of God. This is the divine aspect of religion, and the two together make the world and the activity of the spirit an intelligible whole. The "What is Truth" of jesting Pilate finds here its answer. All truth, all life, all process, in short Reality itself, is known in the knowledge of the creative love which is the activity of spirit. We see sex growing to greater and greater importance until we reach man. Then self-consciousness intervenes; the ideas of relation and of fellowship dawn; love finds a beginning, and then sex begins to lose its privileged place. From pre-eminence it sinks to a secondary position. Its spiritual part is nearly played, and something higher carries on the work. Love is more than passion. Sex must continue to function, for man has still a physical body; but its spiritual significance is understood, and that is a thing far greater than itself. As love grows, passion sinks and sinks from its first prominence, till love is all. "They neither marry nor are given in marriage, but are as the angels." If this means anything at all, it means that in the end the physical body will have played its noble part and pass away, with its passions and its failures; while the life goes on, revealed in a body spiritual.

In the light of this understanding nothing is left unclean. Even in the work of Freud, in so far as it is true, and not coloured by the overstrained interpretations of a pathologist, there is nothing to shock, though much to sadden us. Where in man there is over-emphasis of sex there is a return to the lower, animal stage. Men are regarding life in terms of what has been, and not of what shall be. They are falling short of their own possibilities. In what degree this phenomenon is pathological, due to some neurosis or psychosis, we may not judge them; in what degree their over-concentration on animal passion, to the exclusion of true spiritual activity, is under the control of the will we are in presence of sin. For, from the evolutionary point of view, sin is the refusal to live up to the standard that is at present possible, the acquiescence in a standard that belongs properly to a stage outgrown; lower; more animal, less divine. It is content with an anachronism; the willing acceptance, the welcome of failure to progress—and this means *refusal* to progress[34].

But to see in the sex-impulse the *explanation* of love is to fall into the same error as do the materialists, though the error has assumed a new and more subtle guise. You can no more explain love by sex than you can explain mind by matter. In both cases you are using terms to which you can attach no meaning. Ultimately I

---

self-defence the 'other' is not regarded as in personal relation to the person threatened, at all events in early stages of development; he is as external as a flood or a precipice. Nevertheless in fear and hate, when they have reached a high stage of development, there is a feeling of personal relation. But only in one sense can this relation be termed personal; the 'other' is recognised as a person, but in concentrating our attention on the things in him we fear and hate we concentrate it on his 'otherness'—on his lack of any but an external relation to us. There is nothing reciprocal; we refuse to give or receive. It is this externality of relation that makes hate and fear so poignant and so bitter.

[34] Cf. *Evolution and the Need of Atonement*, ch. IV. *et passim*.

cannot think of matter and yet exclude mind; I cannot think of sex and yet exclude relation, and so, ultimately, love. For scientific purposes no doubt I can do both, for science is a process of abstraction in which we disregard everything that is not relevant to an immediate and narrow purpose. But philosophy may not abstract. She deals with the concrete and the real.

We have apparently lost sight of the question of beauty; but those who have followed the thought of the first chapter will realise that we have not in fact gone far afield. Upon the foundation of sex, as we have seen, the sexless activity of love is being slowly reared; and love is relation—relation is the reciprocal, creative activity which is spirit, and spirit is Reality. God is Love; men perfected are, or will be, love. The being of God and men alike is the activity of personal relationship, made perfect in union while yet each retains his self-identity[35]. The knowledge of this relation, the expression of it, is Beauty; and in Beauty the whole theoretic activity is comprehended in the ultimate resort, when intuition, the immediate contact, and logic, the mediate contact, are made one through perfect knowledge.

Since then, the first origin of the realisation of relationship is born in the sex-impulse, here the beginnings of beauty must be sought. But to search for them in any developed form—to search for what we understand by beauty—in the animal consciousness is vain. There can exist in it only some dim fore-shadowing, some preference. Not until true self-consciousness arises can there be any real sense of beauty, if beauty be the intuition of a relation expressed to the self and to others. And arguing from the psychological effect of beauty upon ourselves—the longing it produces, and the creative impulse—we have been driven to define beauty as the expression of a relation. The germ from which love and beauty will spring is already there in the relation between animals, but who would guess that from the least of seeds should be born so great and noble a tree?

Many have sought the origin of the sense of beauty in the attraction of sex, and have then hanged Beauty under this bad name. To do this is to proclaim oneself a materialist. Our idea is far different. Reasoning from the standpoint to which we are driven by an examination of evolution that does not neglect the phenomenon of personality; finding the only explanation of evolution itself in free personal relationship; we see in sex the primitive ground-work of that relationship. Physically, the sex relation subserves many purposes; it provides a chief mode of introducing variation, it blindly helps on the evolutionary process through selective mating, it provides the chemical stimulus to the development of a new organism from the gamete or sex cell. But it does more. In the light of the end we see in sex a far nobler function; of a significance not transient but abiding. In the great adventure of Creative Love, to sex is given the task of bringing about those relations which constitute the ground-work of the personal union which is Love. Of the understanding and the expression of this relation is born the sense of beauty, destined gradually to transfigure the world for man, as he learns to see order and purpose and significant relation in the whole, and to endure eternal and yet always new.

---

[35] McDowall, *opp. citt. passim.*

CONCLUSION.

Throughout this essay, in our quest for the meaning of Beauty we have been driven to reject the ground of the Natural as the proper standpoint for viewing the Beautiful. Rather, in Nature regarded from the point of view of ultimate Reality, we have found a value only through relation; and it is the intuition of this relation, expressed to conscious mind, that constitutes Beauty. No relation is, however, satisfying but one which is mutual. There is beauty in all expressed relations, even those of mathematics and physics, but because these relations are primarily expressed for the purpose of the science as between thing and thing, and their relation to the perceiving mind is relegated to the background, the sense of beauty is not roused in any great degree. By scenery a far more vivid sense of beauty is kindled, and hand in hand with this goes a keener sense of dissatisfaction and creative longing. By pictures and the like we are brought into touch with the mind of the artist; he has felt a relation and given to it technical expression, and we follow anew his creative intuition. In doing so we get in some degree into relation with his mind as well as with the thing in which he saw beauty; and we derive additional joy from this personal relation, mediate though it be. But still there is dissatisfaction, as well as creative desire. This longing is identical with the longing of one-sided love. We receive and cannot give. Only in perfectly reciprocal love is the longing absent, while yet the creative aspect is most vividly present.

The study of Philosophy irradiates the world for us, increasing our sense of the beauty that is in it. We understand more; the world's relation to us is more real, deeper, wider. Religion has the same effect, though in so far as it sometimes belittles the world it tends also to deaden our understanding of the world's beauty. But if our philosophy coincides with our religion and our scientific theory is a part of both, Beauty has a chance of winning her proper position. If this philosophy and this religion find their ultimate Reality in the personal relationship we call love; if in their 'science' the creative process of that love's activity in self-limitation stands revealed; Beauty indeed comes to her own. In our intuition of the world's beauty we are in touch with the creative idea of the Master Mind. Only a philosophy and a religion that are rooted and grounded in the God who is Love, yet take the fullest account of the time-processes of love which we call evolution, can reveal the fulness of Beauty. Then Beauty is seen as Spirit's grasp upon the relation between all the parts of the whole—a relation that is not yet complete, and can only be complete when the sole relation is that of love between personal beings, of whom God is the first in timeless Being. Then, when matter is seen as the expression of God's self-limitation for the sake of His people's freedom, realisation dawns that matter is instinct with beauty for the understanding mind. Aesthetic becomes the link that binds all our theoretic knowledge together, making it one—serviceable as an equal partner with the practical activity. In this partnership the activity of the spirit is perfected[36]. The beauty of relationship is always new, just as love is always new. Our creation is our expression of our personal being in relationship, which is ultimately love. God's creation is the expression of His Personal Being in relationship. Without relationship He would not be personal; but more is implied in this statement than merely internal relations. Personality, the δύναμις of κοινωνία, is centrifugally creative, as we have seen elsewhere, and the thing created, because it is a relationship, is beautiful, and is new. In the perennial newness of beauty we find the key to God's creative activity. He creates new persons, because His relation to them is new and beautiful. Just because His experience is the experience of Perfect Personality new things are perpetually added. Without this activity His Being would not be perfect. Its perfection is substantiated by its power of finding beauty new. Only the inactive dullard fails to see beauty and is bored, and in his very dulness he loses the prerogative of personality.

From the height of such a conception, standing upon ultimate Reality, we have looked down upon the humble beginnings of the intuition of relation, or of beauty. These we found pre-eminently in sex, and so far we were in accord with the psychoanalytic schools of Vienna and of Zurich. But we saw sex transformed and made beautiful, because our eyes were fixed, not on low, immediate purposes, but on the wonderful things that were to come. Mainly out of the relationship of sex spring music, art, literature—all the beauty that is so far removed from its physical origin—and it is in these things of eternal value that we find the true purpose of sex, as opposed to its immediate physical meaning. In music, art, literature we see the expression of growing understanding. The Reality is brought nearer and nearer to man.

Could Philosophy but bring our thought in closer contact with Aesthetic, as Croce has nobly endeavoured to bring it, understanding would quicken marvellously. Could religion embrace the arts and use them, the world would move Godward with fresh inspiration; the arts themselves would be enriched, coming into their true heritage. Croce has paved the way to understanding, but he missed the goal because he did not perceive that the content of Reality is relationship. This essay attempts to indicate how much is lost by his omission. God is Love; Reality is Love. Love is relationship. Beauty is the expression of our understanding of that relationship. The Good, the True, the Beautiful are seen as different aspects of the same Reality; each definable only in terms of another; each involving, and indeed being, the same system of relations seen from a different angle. Goodness is the relation of spirit to spirit, Truth the relation of part to part and part to whole, Beauty the expression of the spirit's knowledge of the relations that make up Reality. Our understanding of these relations—yes, and God's understanding—is perpetually creative, and its creation is a new thing for Perfect Being; for the Perfection of Being is only substantiated by its power to create the new, the beautiful, the related. Matter is beautiful because it is understood as the expression of the infinite activity

[36] For detailed consideration of the nature of evolutionary process in material conditions reference may be made to my earlier works, to which the present essay constitutes a postscript.

of the spirit of love. As Personal Being is the one thing that lasts beyond Time, and carries in itself the character of absoluteness, so it appears that Beauty, the knowledge and expression of the relationship of Personal Being, is also eternal. Beauty can never cease, for it is a necessary part of God's experience and ours.

APPENDIX:
ART FORMS IN DEVELOPMENT.

Although any detailed treatment of the concrete forms of art is entirely foreign to the intention of this essay, it is desirable that we should devote a little consideration to the way in which these technical expressions arise and to the psychological effects they produce. In doing this we shall refer to the work of various artists, but only for purposes of illustration. The part of the art critic is as unnecessary to our purpose as it is beyond our powers.

To omit all reference to concrete matters seemed undesirable, as leaving the theory rather in the air. On the other hand any detailed discussion of the theory as applied to the development of concrete art-forms must necessarily introduce debatable propositions, and must be tentative. It therefore seemed desirable to relegate the discussion of concrete matters to an Appendix, and to state clearly that what was there said was meant rather to suggest ideas than to lay down definite principles. Applications that may be open to question do not invalidate a theory, while they do make for clear understanding of it.

The question whether beauty itself is a universal or a particular has already found implicit answer. Since beauty is the expression of a relation that is understood as an essential determination of Reality, the concept of beauty is a pure concept. It is expressive, it is concrete, it is universal. It is clearly expressed to the self as a cognitive product, expressible in words (definition) and symbols (technique). It answers to Croce's test that though "universal and transcendent in relation to the single representation, it is yet immanent in the single, and therefore in all representations," and is therefore concrete. It also transcends the single representations, "so that no single representation, and no number of them can be equivalent to the concept" and so is universal.

But the foundation of every universal concept exists in an intuition of the particular. The intuition and its expression to the self come first, then follows the extension of the theoretic activity in logic. The concept of beauty must, then, have arisen, and at every fresh realisation must still arise, like all concepts, from an intuition of Reality as existent in a particular; and we must therefore seek its origin in specific individual cases.

Now we have argued that beauty is most probably associated initially with sex, since with sex the idea of personal relationship first arises. Our main thesis would not however be invalidated if it could be shown that a vague intuition of relation with inorganic or non-personal objects arose first. The intuition of relation may well have several separate starting points. Only, in this case, the reciprocal element would be absent (though its lack might not be felt except as a vague dissatisfaction) and could only arise when the sex-relation was the subject of a similar intuition. But most likely the intuition of relation did arise with sex, and, since our argument is concerned to show that ultimately the intuition of beauty leads to the expression of mutual relationship—love—and finds there the explanation both of its peculiar quality, and of the creative longing it produces, we will confine our argument mainly to this aspect.

Now if this be so, the sense of beauty is likely to be associated in its earliest stages with sight, and only in a secondary degree with sound, in the mating-call and in the beginnings of language. This is borne out by the fact that music usually lags behind, and is more primitive in expression than the visual arts—personal ornamentation and even decoration of objects. True, the first formal *expression* is likely to be in sound—in the beginnings of language. The dynamic relation between persons maybe accompanied and expressed throughout by speech. But at this primitive level it will be a very limited intuition or understanding that is expressed, and moreover, an intuition that is based on visual stimuli. We may therefore leave the question of language for the present. Its importance in the earlier stages is mainly practical. Through sight (when the stage of simple chemiotaxis is passed) arises the perception of desirability in the opposite sex[37], which is the animal starting-point from which love is evolved. This desirability and this relation are expressed to the self, and this expression is beauty in its humblest beginning. Then, later, the creative aspect enters into consciousness. At first it was satisfied, unconsciously, in mating; but soon this unconscious satisfaction is felt to be inadequate. The representative process begins.

Now here we find a difficulty. According to our theory, the earliest attempts at the pictorial art should be pictures of men and women, but this is not, I believe, the case[38]. We must, however, remember that the idea of symbolic magic arises very early. This is natural. The representation of a thing is that thing in some degree. You have power over your representations, therefore you have power over the thing. The use of such power has an anti-social aspect, which forbids its common or public use except in the form, of a magico-religious ceremony. It is unlikely, therefore, that if such representations were made, they should have come down to us. Moreover, it is unnecessary that the magic object should bear any superficial resemblance to the thing it symbolises; indeed it is undesirable that it should be recognisable by others, since the practice for which it is destined is nefarious and illicit. An esoteric significance is enough. There is a very close connection between primitive art and religion. Thus the Palaeolithic drawings of animals in the dark caves of Périgord and Altamira, are undoubtedly connected with magico-religious ceremonies to give power over the beasts. For this reason then—the acquiring of a *prise* over the object represented—we should hardly expect to find many early

---

[37] Even though there may be a mating-call.

[38] I believe that I am right in saying that it is not until the Neolithic period that human (female) images are found, and some of these are probably divinities, though Dr A. C. Haddon informs me that there are Neolithic paintings of human beings on rocks in Spain which presumably do not represent divinities.

drawings of men and women, other than divinities. Even to-day many savages evince the greatest fear of having their likeness drawn. Nevertheless, these Neolithic drawings do exist, proving that there was no universal tabu on such representations. Moreover such drawings as those of the Bushmen show that primitive art at times uses drawings to record historical events, such as raids by other tribes. The comparative scarcity of primitive drawings is, however, easily explicable when we take the fact of magical beliefs into account. And there are sufficiently numerous examples of drawings of animals—bear, rhinoceros, lion, mammoth, bison, reindeer, to show that prehistoric man did have an intuition of his relation to other creatures. Furthermore, since the creative impulse does receive some, if unconscious, satisfaction in sex-relationship, expressed in word and action, there is the less need for technical expression in the early stages. We find at all events enough prehistoric drawings to show the recognition of relation, and the expressive activity, and these are the desiderata for an aesthetic fact.

Leaving the most primitive level, we find the development of decoration. Pottery is shaped with some regard to form and symmetry, and simple ornament of a geometric character makes its appearance[39]. Much might be said on this subject, but we will confine ourselves to a few fundamental consider ations. In the first place we notice that here man's art is practically unfettered by religious and magical inhibitions. Geometric forms do not generally represent any person or power[40]. Artistic creation therefore can move freely. Next, we observe that the art is reaching a higher level, and that consciously. There is conscious elimination and abstraction at work in the construction of patterns made of simple lines and curves. We find also the rudiments of an endeavour to find a harmony and rhythm that may give a sense of satisfied understanding. Men are beginning to feel the need of unity and harmony and order, and in so far as geometric ornament gives the feeling of these and of purpose, it is beautiful, for it expresses their intuition of an ordered reality.

It is unnecessary for us to discuss the intrinsic beauty of curves, or the mental satisfaction afforded by the golden section. The Greeks, and later writers such as Fechner, have expended much ingenuity in doing this. But their conclusions amounted to little more than that the aesthetic pleasure given by geometric form was due to the sense of symmetry and order and unity that were brought about by elaborate differentiation of detail subordinated to a single idea. As we have just said, Geometric ornament expresses man's intuition of an ordered relation and interdependence in Reality.

We have introduced the ideas of elimination and abstraction. These are present in all artistic representation, and probably in all artistic perception. Because the power is rare in any high degree of development, artistic genius is rare. Moreover it frequently happens in ordinary people that the perception of beauty is first

[39] Really, geometric art seems to have arisen nearly contemporaneously with representative art, for patterns of considerable complexity and symmetry are found in the later palaeolithic period.

[40] Though the representation of an eye is frequently included in the pattern as a counter-charm, and indeed many of the patterns *may* originally have had a magical significance, though most seem to be merely inspired by woven basket-work and the like.

aroused consciously by pictures rather than by natural scenes. A flower is simple enough for a child to understand, and we find that in many children, especially artistic ones, the perception of beauty is first awakened by flowers. The elements of a sunset, or a moonlight scene with clear tones and silhouetted outlines, are simple enough for the untrained mind to appreciate. But it requires an artistic genius to see the beauty of a complex landscape. In representing this technically he simplifies, emphasises, eliminates and abstracts. The man who looks at his picture follows the creative process of his mind, and, the elimination being already done for him, is able to appreciate. Moreover he receives training in the process, and is the more ready to eliminate for himself; to appreciate natural beauty of a complex order. Even if our artistic development is not high, we love pictures because in looking at them and understanding them we perform a creative act ourselves; but it is the artist who has made it possible for us to perform the act by his simplification of the problem. Browning clearly understood this, for he wrote:

> We're made so that we love
> First, when we see them painted, things we have passed
> Perhaps a hundred times nor cared to see[41].

Sometimes the artist achieves his emphasis by means not wholly agreeable to the medium which he is using. Many artists of great technical ability link human sympathies with an admirably interpretative *mise-en-scène* which carries out their vision. Nevertheless the picture that tells a story calls in adventitious aid. It is like the illustrated reading book of a child; by the child mind it is created, and to the child mind it appeals. It cannot express a clear intuition by a simple representation in a single medium, but uses two, appealing not only in pictorial symbols, but in dramatic as well, and the intuition itself is obscured by the process. Owing to this confusion of media and of intuition the result is unsatisfactory to minds more developed aesthetically, for reasons that we shall adduce later, while yet the double appeal makes the meaning more evident to the beginner. Again certain landscape artists of the second rank by insistence on simple elements of natural beauty, by emphasis, and by elimination of distracting ideas, open a new vision to minds hardly prepared yet for such intuition in face of the natural object. Add to this the half conscious yet acutely pleasurable process of following out the technical means by which the artist has impressed his intuition upon canvas, and we can understand the joy of looking at their pictures.

But where the artist's vision goes deeper, where the reality is more clearly seen, and where in order to express this intuition, to represent it, and to bring out its less obvious harmony and order, a more sweeping process of elimination and abstraction is needed, the simple mind is unable to follow. Not everyone is at the stage to appreciate the subtle symphonies of Whistler, the bare simplicity of D. Y. Cameron, the rigorous certainty of Botticelli. The conventions and purposeful line of an early Japanese print; the vibrant light of the post-impressionist landscape artists; the wilful, obtrusive, almost harsh insistence of the cubist that you *shall* turn your mind away from curves that hitherto you have deemed essential, in order to grasp other truths, not only seem ugly—that is to say, meaningless—to

---

[41] *Fra Lippo Lippi.*

the mind whose artistic perception is little developed, but may even distract it, in rebellious protest, from the truth the artist wishes to proclaim, though others further advanced find in some of their work a very high type of beauty. And, be it added, the artist himself fails in his expression if he overdoes the emphasis in such a way that his representation of the Reality becomes lopsided and inharmonious, as is too often the case. Further where he is not a creative artist at all, but a slavish imitator of a method not really his own, we are presented with the meaningless monstrosities that here and there defile the Salon des Indépendants—and other less catholic exhibitions! In some, too, the animal basis is the only intuition expressed, and art gobbles greedily at its mess of pottage.

Yet as a whole we have moved a long way from the animal expression of a need of its complementary animal. The whole world is related to us, and in that relation we find beauty. And beautiful as it is we find it very lovable, even though we cannot but feel that our love can never be satisfied since we can give nothing back.

Yet something we can give, though not to it—something that makes things clearer. In our minds we can give to this world a meaning, as itself subordinate, yet the necessary means of our self-realisation, and we can share this meaning with others. We find a meaning in life, and that meaning is fellowship. We find a meaning in nature, and that meaning dwells in the Creative Being of the God who is Love. Beauty, more clearly day by day, becomes for us the expression of Reality, and that Reality is the reciprocal relationship of persons. Religion gives one pathway of approach, Beauty another, but both join to form the highway of our God. There is more than room for beauty in religion; there is more than room for aesthetic in theology; there is an absolute need, if they are not to be in a measure inexpressive, lopsided, and therefore ugly. Our concept of Reality must be symmetrical, or fail of adequacy.

What is true of pictorial art is equally true of other forms. Style—the higher art of language—demands education before it can be appreciated. In literature again, the general public prefers Longfellow to Keats, *The Passing of Arthur* to *A Death in the Desert*, Ella Wheeler Willcox to the *Divina Commedia*. Henry James demands a more intimate appreciation of the spirit of man than does Dickens. In all these there is beauty—the expression of an intuition—but those who see furthest and most clearly have the smallest public. Most men cannot even follow where they lead, and few indeed are the pioneers.

Before we leave the question of literature and language, we may just glance at its development. This is comparatively an easy matter to understand. The warning, the expression of satisfaction, the mating-call are common among animals. The powers of communication and of speech develop with the development of self-consciousness. They are expressions of the relation between the self and its 'others,' and especially of the relation between the self and other selves. They carry the germs of understanding, and as they lead from the particular to the more general they bear in them the quality of the beautiful. The relations between the self and the other selves, and between the self and the environment, become more and more universalised. In speech they are communicated, but speech is transient. A more permanent record is required, and here again resort is had to symbolism, less generally intelligible, more esoteric, than the pictorial symbol, since there is no one universal language; the symbolism of written speech. Speech, however, is episodic and dramatic. It moves along with the march of events. So too with literature, for the most part. The Pictorial and Plastic arts represent beauty as static; yet they are not lifeless. Activity, movement, is implicit in them, while yet the beauty they express is restful, and has in it something of the quality of absoluteness and transcendence. Language, literature, drama are dynamic. In them beauty moves; immanent and unquiet at first sight; yet here too there is something that expresses the eternal meaning. Purpose moves to its fulfilment, and, while it moves, the end is in view. Nevertheless in pictorial art the static side is the most prominent, in linguistic the dynamic side. We may observe, however, that in order to counteract the transitoriness of purely episodic speech, recourse is had to visual symbolism as well. The graphic art aims at perpetuating the episode, and by doing so renders possible the development to which we shall immediately draw attention.

Now the untrained mind appreciates the dynamic aspect of literature, whether it be the originative mind or the mind of the reader. This explains the output and the popularity of the thrilling tale of adventure. At its lowest we find the Penny Dreadful. Through Stanley Weyman and Dumas we move towards Conrad and Meredith and Hardy, where the dynamic element is thrillingly present (as present it must be indeed even in the most quiet essays) but where it is subordinated to a clear vision of the permanent and eternal which we have mis-termed static. In poetry this truth is obvious. Even in drama, though our attention is distracted by the action, it is the chief quality if the drama is really great. In Sophocles, in Euripides, in Shakespeare; perhaps almost too consciously in Galsworthy, and Paul Claudel and Synge, for conscious art loses the sincerity of a first vision; it is not the episodic sequence that interests us, except from the point of view of technique. Our attention is focussed upon the motive, the fundamental intuition to which the dramatist is trying to give technical expression. Moreover in all the infinite variety of literary art the motive is the same. One definite intuition is expressed—that of relationship; relation between person and person, relation between person and machine, relation between person and some ever-ruling Order, be it Fate, Chance, or God also personal. It is the reality of personal inter-relationship that underlies all literature, be it love-poem, novel, or some drama of Fate in which personal relationship is overshadowed by the impersonal, or at least the unsympathetic; or else it is the one-sided relation of a person to a thing, as in descriptive science, which has only the beauty of order. But can we say that the intuition which the pictorial artist represents is the same as this? Hardly, unless the picture tells a story; and in so far as it does this we feel that the realm of pictorial art is invaded by an alien influence. It may at first sight seem surprising that art should not gain by the introduction of various intuitions of relation; that it does not, as a rule, is certain. All the arts overlap; we shall see the most marked example of this when we come to consider music and deal further with this point; but intrinsically each is peculiar in its scope and method.

Now it is worth while to observe that the longing aroused by the beauty of literature is rather different from that induced by pictures. It is less vague. Because literature deals with the relation between persons our attention is directed towards the persons we know—our longings and aspirations reach out consciously towards them and towards God. We think of particular people and our relation to them. Our creative longing is directed towards them, in active relation, or towards creative literary work of which, more or less consciously to ourselves they are the background. Moreover we always identify ourselves, in a greater or less degree, with one or more of the protagonists of the story; in them we suffer, we love, we adventure at second-hand. This phenomenon of identification, closely allied as it is to day-dreaming, has of late come much under the attention of psychoanalysts under the title of phantasy; a term covering all attempts to achieve through the imagination the satisfaction denied to us in actual life. For our present purpose this is only noteworthy as confirming the truth of our observation that in literary creation, whether at first or second hand, it is human relation—the relation of ourselves and others—that lies behind our intuition and its expression.

In some pictorial art this relation between persons, this personal touch, does not obtain. In landscape the artist's intuition obviously deals with the relation of things to men—a relation much more onesided. Correspondent to this, we find our intuition and our longing far more vague, far more dissatisfied. There needs a higher knowledge of Reality to understand how man has relation to things. The intuition of this relation is generally expressed with far less understanding. Human relations may intrude, and we get the story-picture and the problem-picture. Moral relations may intrude, and we get the symbolic picture, such as those of Watts and Blake. Drama, myth and legend may intrude and we get the Ladies of Shallot, the Ledas, and the Calumnies of Apelles.

But pictorial art reaches its highest plane in the religious picture and the portrait. Have we not, here, the intrusion of the story in the first case; and in the second have we not the purely human relations between artist and sitter?

I think it is just to say that the religious picture is not episodic. It represents what, for want of a better word, we have termed a static intuition. In the greatest Madonnas, even those of the beginning of the decadence, such as Raphael's, all the birth-pangs, all the pain, and all the achievement of life at its highest go to make up the intuition of the artist. I venture to think that in one picture at least, the Madonna of the Magnificat, the artist even hints subtly that he is expressing in an image the whole meaning of the world, by distorting his figures and modifying his lights as they would be distorted and modified when reflected in a convex mirror. διὰ κάτοπτρον is for all art, but the fact is not evident to him who only glances. The artist's intuition must be understood, by a mind that follows it creatively; even if its creation be at times over-ingenious.

The religious picture, no doubt, could not have been painted but for the historic episode which it represents. But there is a strong presumption that it does not owe its intuition to one episode, nor even to the whole history of a life; though a Crucifixion, an Entombment, and indeed a Madonna, would only be intelligible in their fulness to one who knew the life of Christ. It is the relation of a whole Life, Divine yet Human, to the life of each one of us that lies at the bottom of the artist's vision. Only a great Christian can paint a great Madonna, however sin-stained he may be. Magdalene, who loved much, could see deeper than jesting Pilate, deeper than the self-righteous Pharisee.

There is here no intrusion of an alien element; a vision of Reality is represented in one medium. The episode no doubt is there, but it is incidental, and does not constitute the vision. Episode is always there, even in a landscape; the question is whether the appeal—the original intuition—is episodic or universal. But no doubt the human relation is emphasised; and in this respect we have moved far away from landscape. The relation of man to inanimate nature is however included and interpreted in the artist's vision. I think that the half-conscious perception of this lies behind the frequent introduction of landscape in such pictures. It may be said that these simply help to complete the composition, but to say this is to beg the question. Why do they complete the composition? Why do they satisfy us? Is it not that they form an intrinsic part of the artist's intuition; that in the harmony of figures and landscape he symbolises, and we after him, the universal harmony which he has seen?

In a portrait, too, we read not only the relation between sitter and artist, which must be a relation of deep sympathy and understanding if the portrait is to be anything but an imitation, but also the relation of the sitter to all the events of his life. Think of Raeburn's portrait of James Wardrop. The strength, the kindliness, the rugged purpose, the humour with which the old man faced his life all through are there. It is the face of a man who has fought and won, and in fighting and winning has learned much wisdom. Think of Giorgione's Portrait of a Gentleman, with its wealth of refinement; with its conviction that "manners makyth man," sustained with gentleness already many times when courtesy and calm were not easy. Yet here too there is no representation of episode. The painter's art is faithful to itself and allows no alien intrusion. The harmony, the unity of a man's life, compounded though that life be of sequent episodes, makes the artist's intuition. History has become philosophy. An absolute thing, an aspect of Reality, is presented, and we feel somehow that it is not set against the world but includes the world.

The same kind of thing may be said of lapidary art, and we will not dwell on it in detail. The sculptor sees beauty in the human or animal form and in three dimensional representation generalises from it, whether his work represent an individual or an ideal; for the individual is used to express an ideal, the ideal is localised in an individual. The problem of the architect is somewhat different, being on the theoretic side the attempt to portray in three dimensions that which the designer of geometric patterns expresses in two—rhythm and order; multiplicity that establishes a unity; unity that interprets a multiplicity. But here, more than in other arts, the practical has to be kept in mind, and a harmony preserved between the economic and the theoretic activities. Generally one or other predominates, no one clear idea is expressed, and in consequence, much modern architecture, especially domestic and civic architecture, is unpleasing. To build a house is harder than to paint a picture, because men have to live in a house; and in a contention between two ideas the artistic side is overbalanced by the practical. Moreover the idea of relationship is comparatively subordinate here just because two ideas are set over against one another. The relationship of a thing to a man is in view. The aim is primarily economic, and beauty takes a second place because the intuition of harmony is vague and its expression imperfect.

If, however, a house is built, as some Tudor and Georgian houses were, with an eye to simple proportion which must not be violated, but otherwise with the realisation that it had to be lived in, and that it must be designed solely with this end in view, the result is eminently pleasing. There is no falsity, no attempt to mingle irreconcileables, no striving after a beauty that cannot be achieved because it is without meaning in such a connection.

We may now turn to music, in some ways the most difficult of all. Beginning with the evolutionary aspect, as with linguistic art we find its origin in the relation of beasts to each other and to the world. The mating-call, the crooning of passion and of satisfied well-being, the warning of danger, the hunting call, the sound of the wind, the sea, the river, the "going in the tops of the trees," provide the ground-work of both, expressing the relation of beast to beast, and beast to thing. But, as we have seen, such calls, such sounds, and the language to which they give rise, are episodic. The sense of unity and endurance is lost. Just as, over against the visual symbols of episode which constitute the beginnings of literature we find the visual symbols of unity and static endurance which characterise pictorial art, so too we find the auditory symbols of episode that make speech, and the auditory symbols of unity that make music. We saw that, to preserve the episode of speech, visual symbolism is eventually called in. Even to-day the untrained reader has to form the sound with his lips as he reads; for the more expert the visual symbol definitely represents the sound: the written symbols have their own timbre. So too with music. To preserve the unity from being lost, it comes at last to be symbolised visually, and there are many who can hear the music as they read the score. Both the letter on the page and the notes on the stave are symbols of the second degree—symbols of symbols—for what they symbolise is in itself the symbol of the artist's intuition of a unity in multiplicity. This in parenthesis.

We have said that in purely episodic sound such as the danger-call and the mating-call the sense of unity is absent. Doubtless no call is really and wholly episodic, in man at any rate, but it cannot be questioned that the episode is predominant. The sense of relation is transient; the economic need is all important.

But the theoretic activity cannot be left out of account for long. The man of to-day, when he feels his whole being in harmony, his body tingling from the cold bath, sings lustily. When we are well and cheerful we sing. So too when a bird is well and cheerful, with all his bodily needs satisfied or soon to be satisfied—so readily satisfied as to be themselves a pleasure of anticipation—he sings. No doubt the cave-mother sang to her baby in quiet murmurs; no doubt the cave-father hummed as he lolled in the cave-mouth after dinner, idly binding an arrow-head upon the shaft. Somehow, in a rhythmic sequence of sound the satisfaction of a body in harmonious rhythm with itself and its surroundings is expressed. Then, we may imagine, the singer becomes aware of his song, and begins to think about it. The beauty of the song as a whole, the beauty of a sequence in sound that makes a unity, is consciously perceived, and a new art dawns. It is an art very similar to that of the designer of geometric patterns. Unity is established through infinite multiplicity of details, in forming no one of which is the unity forgotten. The music mirrors an intuition of harmony in a Reality that owes its unity to its multiplicity and its multiplicity to its unity; a Reality that is based on relationship of parts.

In music, then, we find rhythm, order, sequence. It is both episodic and static, though episode and unity are in symbolic form. In the individual sequences, the internal multiplicity, the episode is given; in the whole, the unity of Reality, the static, or better, the absolute element.

Because in good music these two aspects must of necessity be perfectly balanced, music can rouse the keenest, highest sense of beauty in a greater degree than any other of the arts.

But often music falls short of this. Mendelssohn for instance, too often sacrifices everything to prettiness. The individual sequences are trivial and empty. Multiplicity of episode is lost sight of in a rather petty unity; the two are not balanced. The fourth sound is simply a fourth note, not a star. Not only is the intuition limited, but the balance is not preserved between the notes and the whole in its expression. Bach owes his pre-eminence to the perfect balance between attention to detailed sequence and expression of a great intuition. Future musicians may see further than he did, but unless they can achieve his perfect balance they will fail to express what they see, and in so far as they fail they will be rewarded with ugliness.

The music-hall tune has but a very paltry vision to express; generally the relationship it portrays is one of vulgar intrigue or animal desire, at best one of elementary aspiration; and its notes have a purely subordinate and utilitarian *rôle*. If it is pretty or ingenious it has got far beyond the average. Generally, moreover, it is constrained by considerations alien to music. The words are written, and the tune has to illustrate them. In this it differs from folk-tunes, where words and music grow together, each shaping, moulding, modifying the other, till the song is one thing.

This brings us back to a question which we have several times touched upon, and as often shelved—the question of the overlapping of different arts. Opera, oratorio, and ballet give us excellent examples, and from them we will draw the material of our brief discussion.

In Opera we have drama, episode expressed in language, set in a more or less accordant scene with histrionic accompaniment, and woven in with a musical interpretation. In Oratorio we have the same thing without the scenery and the histrionics. In Ballet—and of this art the Russian Ballet is especially in my mind—we have the drama, the scene, the histrionic accompaniment in choregraphic form, and the music.

Let us take Opera first. There are two appeals to the ear and two to the eye. The music and the words; the acting and the scenery. The scenery, if subdued and perfectly in accord with the action, does not much distract the attention, for it is purely a pictorial setting. Nevertheless a sense is growing that in drama it ought to be so much subordinated that it does not distract the attention at all, being confined to a few patterns that help in our understanding of the motive, or to simple draperies. As far as I am aware this has not yet been attempted in opera[42], but opera is such a jumble of incongruities that it can never be an artistic whole, much as we may rejoice in individual parts of it. The words, however, do constrain the music in a manner thoroughly unjustifiable: "In composing an opera the stage should be the musician's first thought, he must not abuse the confidence of the theatre-goer who comes to *see* as well as to *hear*.... The stage often paralyses a composer's inspiration, that is why symphonic and chamber music are so far superior to opera. A symphony or a sonata imposes no limitations, but in opera, the first necessity is to speak the musical language of the great public[43]." Moreover the action and the music are so incompatible that we are forced to leave our sense of humour outside the theatre door. When the hero explains for ten minutes that the heroine is in acute danger and that therefore he must hurry away; when Tristan and Isolde sing their passion with complete detachment for more than half an hour; we cannot feel that the action helps the music or the music the action. In Oratorio, since action is absent, we feel this particular incongruity less, for we manage mentally to eliminate time; but few will be found to defend the oratorio as a form of aesthetic expression. It is the anthem prolonged into a "useless Alexandrine," "which like a wounded snake drags its slow length along." The fatal fact about opera and oratorio is that the music is constrained to do something that is alien to itself. It is interpretive of episode, and the episode forces it into shape. It is not free. This is the root trouble always when two arts overlap. Art must be completely free to express its intuition technically, subject only to the inevitable restrictions of the technique proper to it. From *these* restrictions it even gains, since the lines of simplification are to some extent determined, and this very determination helps the artist towards clear expression of a clear intuition. It would, of course, be absurd to say that music does not express definite intuitions that are expressible through other media as well. "I do not in the least agree with you that music cannot interpret the universal nature of love," writes Tchaikovsky to Nadejda von Meck. "On the contrary, I think only music is capable of doing so. You say words are necessary. O no! This is just where words are not needed, and where they have no power; a more eloquent language comes in, which is music. Look at the poetical forms to which poets have recourse in order to sing of love; they simply usurp the spheres which belong inseparably to music. Words clothed in poetical forms cease to be mere words; they become partly music[44]." But if there is a restriction alien to the art and imposed from without, which prevents full expression in that medium, the result is bound to be more or less a failure. The dramatic episode and the verbal form in opera constitute such a restriction, introducing a vein of unreality that is fatal to aesthetic expression. In oratorio, where the words demand a representation they do not get, and where yet the music is bound by the words, we feel the same thing. Even to take a poem and set it to music is almost bound to lead to aesthetic disappointment. The intuition of the artist is not single nor free. The writer of the melody may recreate the intuition of the poet, he may try to ex-

[42] I understand that Purcell's *Fairy Queen* has just been played at Cambridge with draped scenes only.

[43] Tchaikovsky, letter to N. F. von Meck, Nov. 27th, 1879.

[44] Tchaikovsky, letter to N. F. von Meck, Feb. 9th, 1878.

press the same intuition in his setting, but the setting is none the less constrained by the words. The musician is not at liberty to form one clear intuition and give it free play[45]. The form of the expression is already fixed in part, and the knowledge of this fixation forms a second intuition which generally obscures and confuses the main one. Moreover both expressions appeal to the same sense, that of hearing, and this, apparently, produces greater confusion, more lack of clarity, in the auditor. The same fact accounts for the unsatisfactoriness of music which moves out of its proper sphere and endeavours to tell a definite story or paint a definite scene. The 1812 Overture, fine though it is, can never be said to be pre-eminent as music; nor can Haydn's Creation, nor any of the music that, intentionally or unintentionally, is not single-hearted, but calls up visual images as well as depending on them. This statement does not constitute an indictment of programme-music. The *Adagio* of Beethoven's Fourth Symphony cannot be thus lightly dismissed[46]. In Tchaikovsky's introspective letters we find most interesting accounts of the inspiration from which he worked, and an eloquent defence of programme-music in general, and his own Fourth Symphony in particular[47]. To N. F. von Meck he writes[48]: "Laroche is entirely opposed to a programme. He thinks the composer should leave the hearer to interpret the meaning of the work as he pleases; that the programme limits his freedom; that music is incapable of expressing the concrete phenomena of the physical and mental world.... If you care to hear my opinion on the subject, I will give it in a few words.... I think the inspiration of a symphonic work can be of two kinds: subjective or objective. In the first instance it expresses the personal emotion of joy or sorrow, as when a lyric poet lets his soul flow out in verse. Here a programme is not only unnecessary, but impossible. It is very different when the composer's inspiration is stirred by the perusal of some poem, or by the sight of a fine landscape, and he endeavours to express his impressions in musical forms. In this case a programme is indispensable.... To my mind, both kinds of music have their *raison d'être*, and I cannot understand those who will only admit one of these styles. Of course every subject is not equally suitable for a symphony, any more than for an opera; but, all the same, programme-music can and must exist. Who would insist, in literature, upon ignoring the epic and admitting only the lyric element?"

Tchaikovsky seems to me to ignore the deepest side of music, however; that intuition of an ordered, universal harmony which gives to Bach his pre-eminence. Programme-music, then, is not necessarily limited to any great extent by that which it represents, provided the representation is sufficiently generalised to allow the music free scope. But it is always in danger of losing touch with the universal in over-emphasis of the particular, becoming constrained by its subject. Moreover it loses something of the freedom, and independence of phenomenal existence, which is the peculiar privilege of music and its unique prerogative among

[45] Tchaikovsky's letters to N. F. von Meck give an interesting insight into the process by which the intuition comes to the composer, and his method of working it out. See especially the letters of Feb. 17th, March 5th, and June 24th, 1878.

[46] If one can say that it has a programme and not simply an inspiration.

[47] Letter to Taneiev, March 27th, 1878.

[48] Dec. 5th, 1878.

the arts, taking on something that belongs to painting or language. In so far as the wrong technical medium is used, just so far aesthetic expression fails.

These strictures do not apparently apply, at any rate in the same degree, where two media appealing to two different senses are used simultaneously. We are accustomed to correlate sight and hearing and to form through them a single intuition. This may explain the extraordinary satisfyingness of the Russian Ballet, in spite of its frequent artificiality and the perverted themes and imagery that pass unnoticed by the more healthy-minded public of England. The episodic side, made rhythmical and ordered in its choregraphic presentation, parallels, but does not constrain in any great degree, the musical side. In Les Sylphides especially the same intuition is expressed in two media. The choregraphic artist has studied and followed out the intuition of Chopin, and has expressed it in a different medium. But music and dancing have much ground in common, and consequently both are capable of serving as the technical medium for one or the same intuition. Therefore Les Sylphides[49] is more of an artistic whole than almost any other compound aesthetic expression. Art must be free, and if it use two media, both must express the same intuition—this is the root of the matter. You may appeal simultaneously to two senses, but you must do so in the medium proper to each sense and the intuition must be capable of expression in those media. To appeal to one sense through the medium proper to another is to court disaster. We see that this must be so if, as is the case, the aesthetic intuition has to be founded on the particular before it can move out to discover the universal; and the particular cannot be faithfully represented if the representation is not as clear-cut as the intuition and the reality intuited. Art must be free, for it is the intuition of a relation free on one side at least, and not finally satisfied till it finds rest in mutuality, love, free on both sides. It is the expression of our growing understanding of the meaning of Reality.

No doubt music, like all other arts, has been transformed from its original character. It is no longer imitative, though it may have been first roused by imitative attempts; it is no longer dependent on the harmony of bodily well-being, though it may first have expressed such harmony. In it spirit calls to spirit, no longer body to body. But this need not surprise us. The foundations contribute nothing to the beauty of a building, though upon them the building is reared. All that is greatest in man had a very humble beginning. Even his limbs and lungs had a plebeian ancestry.

We have said nothing of the aesthetic problem of simple tone and colour. Though Plato, and even Hegel, discussed these, it is generally accepted to-day that they do not in fact exist in isolation from other suggestions. They always derive a value from their suggested relations and cannot be conceived apart from these. Such aesthetic value as clear tones and colours have is due to the fact that the elements they suggest and imply are few, like a sunset sky, and therefore they do not demand any great degree of elimination in the mind of the observer.

Neither have we dealt with the problem of the relative importance of colour and form, except implicitly. The essential factor here is, of course, that colour does

---

[49] Petrouchka is said to be equally homogeneous, but I have not seen it, and Carnaval approaches this level.

not exist *per se*. You cannot isolate a thing from its colour, in aesthetic intuition. To begin with, colour is the basis of visual perception, for the light by means of which the eye perceives an object must be of some definite series of wave-lengths of certain amplitudes balanced against one another in some definite manner through the selective absorption of that object, and wave-length is the physical basis of colour. Then, secondly, colour belongs to, and is an integral part of form. Form is not mere shape; it is determined by tone (or wave-amplitude) and colour (or wave-frequency) as well as by outline; and these are essential factors in the unity and order of the whole, and so are essential factors of the intuition.

What we have said, then, of symmetry and geometric form, and of clearness of expression, together with what we have said of the elimination that is involved in aesthetic intuition, really covers the problem.

Together, yet each in its own way, colour and form arouse in us the sense of unity and appeal to us as being in harmony with the intuition derived from other particulars; that in the world, under all its apparent multiplicity, there subsists a unity which relates all things together.

Lector House believes that a society develops through a two-fold approach of continuous learning and adaptation, which is derived from the study of classic literary works spread across the historic timeline of literature records. Therefore, we aim at reviving, repairing and redeveloping all those inaccessible or damaged but historically as well as culturally important literature across subjects so that the future generations may have an opportunity to study and learn from past works to embark upon a journey of creating a better future.

This book is a result of an effort made by Lector House towards making a contribution to the preservation and repair of original ancient works which might hold historical significance to the approach of continuous learning across subjects.

HAPPY READING & LEARNING!

LECTOR HOUSE LLP
E-MAIL: lectorpublishing@gmail.com